AKB48

33 1/3 Global

33 1/3 Global, a series related to but independent from **33 1/3**, takes the format of the original series of short, music-based books and brings the focus to music throughout the world. With initial volumes focusing on Japanese and Brazilian music, the series will also include volumes on the popular music of Australia/Oceania, Europe, Africa, the Middle East, and more.

33 1/3 Japan

Series Editor: Noriko Manabe

Spanning a range of artists and genres-from the 1970s rock of Happy End to technopop band Yellow Magic Orchestra, the Shibuya-kei of Cornelius, classic anime series *Cowboy Bebop*, J-Pop/EDM hybrid Perfume, and vocaloid star Hatsune Miku—**33 1/3 Japan** is a series devoted to in-depth examination of Japanese popular music of the twentieth and twenty-first centuries.

Published Titles:
Supercell's *Supercell* by Keisuke Yamada
Yoko Kanno's *Cowboy Bebop Soundtrack* by Rose Bridges
Perfume's *Game* by Patrick St. Michel

Forthcoming titles:
Cornelius's *Fantasma* by Martin Roberts
Joe Hisaishi's *My Neighbor Totoro: Soundtrack* by Kunio Hara
Nenes' *Koza Dabasa* by Henry Johnson
Shonen Knife's *Happy Hour* by Brooke McCorkle

33 1/3 Brazil

Series Editor: Jason Stanyek

Covering the genres of samba, tropicália, rock, hip hop, forró, bossa nova, heavy metal and funk, among others, **33 1/3 Brazil** is a series devoted to in-depth examination of the most important Brazilian albums of the twentieth and twenty-first centuries.

Published Titles:
Caetano Veloso's *A Foreign Sound* by Barbara Browning
Tim Maia's *Tim Maia Racional Vols. 1 &2* by Allen Thayer
João Gilberto and Stan Getz's *Getz/Gilberto* by Brian McCann

Forthcoming titles:
Dona Ivone Lara's *Sorriso Negro* by Mila Burns
Gilberto Gil's *Refazenda* by Marc A. Hertzman
Milton Nascimento and Lô Borges's *The Corner Club* by Jonathon Grasse
Racionais MCs' *Sobrevivendo no Inferno* by Marília Gessa and Derek Pardue
Jorge Ben Jor's *África Brasil* by Frederick J. Moehn
Naná Vasconcelos's *Saudades* by Daniel B. Sharp

33 1/3 Europe

Series Editor: Fabian Holt
Spanning a range of artists and genres, **33 1/3 Europe** offers engaging accounts of popular and culturally significant albums of Continental Europe and the North Atlantic from the 20th and 21st centuries.

Forthcoming Titles:
Modeselektor's *Happy Birthday* by Sean Nye
Heiner Müller and Heiner Goebbels's *Wolokolamsker Chaussee* by Philip V. Bohlman
Ivo Papasov's *Balkanology* by Carol Silverman
Darkthrone's *A Blaze in the Northern Sky* by Ross Hagen

AKB48

Patrick W. Galbraith and
Jason G. Karlin

Noriko Manabe, Series Editor

BLOOMSBURY ACADEMIC
NEW YORK · LONDON · OXFORD · NEW DELHI · SYDNEY

BLOOMSBURY ACADEMIC
Bloomsbury Publishing Inc
1385 Broadway, New York, NY 10018, USA
50 Bedford Square, London, WC1B 3DP, UK

BLOOMSBURY, BLOOMSBURY ACADEMIC and the Diana logo are
trademarks of Bloomsbury Publishing Plc

First published in the United States of America 2020

Cover design: Louise Dugdale
Cover image: The 7th Annual AKB48 General Election held in Fukuoka,
Japan on June 6, 2015. Courtesy of the Yomiuri Shimbun.

Library of Congress Cataloging-in-Publication Data
Names: Galbraith, Patrick W. author | Karlin, Jason G. author.
Title: AKB48 / Patrick W. Galbraith and Jason G. Karlin.
Description: New York, NY: Bloomsbury Academic, 2019. |
Series: 33 1/3 Japan | Includes bibliographical references and index.
Identifiers: LCCN 2019015848 | ISBN 9781501341106 (hardback:
alk. paper) | ISBN 9781501341113 (pbk. : alk. paper)
Subjects: LCSH: AKB 48 (Musical group) | Girl groups
(Musical groups)–Japan. | Celebrities–Japan. | Celebrities in popular
culture–Japan.
Classification: LCC ML421.A343 G35 2019 | DDC 782.4216/30952–dc23
LC record available at https://lccn.loc.gov/2019015848

ISBN: HB: 978-1-5013-4110-6
PB: 978-1-5013-4111-3
ePDF: 978-1-5013-4113-7
eBook: 978-1-5013-4112-0

Series: 33 1/3 Japan

Typeset by Deanta Global Publishing Services, Chennai
Printed and bound in the United States of America

Contents

Illustrations

Figures

Election held at Ajinomoto Stadium in Tokyo on June 7, 2014.
Source: *Documentary of AKB48 The Time Has Come: Shōjo-tachi wa, ima, sono senaka ni nani wo omou?*, Blu-Ray, directed by Takahashi Eiki (Tokyo: Tōhō, 2014) 62

Tables

Note on Japanese Names and Words

Japanese names are generally listed surname first, as is the custom in Japanese, unless the person publishes under, is generally known by, or prefers the reverse. Japanese words are transliterated according to modified Hepburn romanization. For this reason, macrons appear over some long vowels; however, for words commonly written without macrons in English (e.g., Tokyo), we follow the convention of omitting them.

Introduction

During the first days of school at universities in Japan, young men and women come out to recruit members for their clubs, which are organized around extracurricular activities. On one such campus in the spring of 2018, there was a curious sight to behold. A young man held in his arms a large cardboard box overflowing with CDs—dozens upon dozens of them, the plastic cases piled up and weighing him down as he maneuvered through the crowd. He was giving them away as an advertisement for his club, which was focused on the appreciation of "idols" (*aidoru*). When approached, the young man proudly revealed that he bought all the CDs at full price. Looking into the box, the surprise was not only the sheer volume of CDs but also the fact that many of them were copies of the same single. They appeared in pristine condition, opened, but the CDs inside untouched. He did not buy the CDs to listen to them, the young man confided, but rather to support his idols. Giving the CDs away is another way to do that, too. It's a promotion for them as much as for his club, a way to recruit people into the fold. Passing out a CD, he nodded and moved on.

The CD, like all the rest in the box, was a recording of a song by AKB48, the most commercially successful female artist or group in Japan.[1] Its members are a ubiquitous presence on television, in magazines and commercials, and their music can be heard at stores and gatherings across the country, but this is common with idols more generally and not specifically how they sold the most singles ever by a female artist or group. Year after year, AKB48 releases new singles that each sell over a million copies.[2] The group doesn't necessarily reach these milestones through global circulation or even sales to a broad national demographic. No, AKB48 does it by mobilizing loyal fans like that young Japanese man with his cardboard box full of CDs. The fact that fans are a great market is not news, and media producers and advertisers know that deploying idols will move fans to tune in, show up, and put money down. Using the example of the television series *American Idol*, Henry Jenkins highlights "affective economics," or building, developing, and maintaining relationships to shape desires and impact purchasing decisions (Jenkins 2006: 61–62). The transnational triumph of South Korean idols such as BTS, who topped the Billboard charts in North America in 2018, is a testament to the power of affective relations with fans and the changing face of the music industry.[3] Returning to that young Japanese man with his cardboard box full of CDs, though, it is the aggressive materiality and persistent localness of AKB48 fandom that stands out. Indeed, what is happening with idols such as AKB48 in Japan does seem different from idols such as BTS in South Korea and beyond (Parc and Kawashima 2018). Although the strategy is different, it is no less successful.

To begin, the music does not seem to be the main thing. That young Japanese man did not buy all those CDs, copies of the same CD, because of the music. He listens to the music downloaded and played back on a portable device. He doesn't need even one CD, let alone dozens of copies of the same one. He doesn't listen to any of the CDs, which are dead weight that he found a use for in literally giving away. The music recorded on the CDs matters a whole lot less than the relationship between the idols and this fan, who purchased them to support one member of AKB48 in particular. This may well be why it is so difficult for music lovers and critics to write about AKB48, whose members are often dismissed as inferior singers and disposable products. In the process of judging idols as musicians, or excluding them because they are not, we miss much of what is actually going on. The idols of AKB48 are not inferior or disposable to that young Japanese man. They are also representatives of a whole media-commodity system that we need to understand to appreciate just how superb they are as idols. It is not that one cannot analyze the songs in compelling ways, as Sakakura Shōhei demonstrates in his excellent book on AKB48, but that this endeavor begins with realizing that they are subordinate to a larger "marketing strategy" (Sakakura 2014: 28).

Around the world, CD sales are declining and the economic returns on digital downloads are uncertain, due to what critics call piracy and advocates call peer-to-peer sharing. Since 2015, online streaming services and digital sales have been the music industry's biggest revenue source, overtaking physical format sales. Yet musicians have evidently not benefited from the new era of streaming, receiving just 12 percent of the US$43 billion that the US music industry generated in 2017.[4] Rather than making money solely off of the sale of music itself, musicians find that touring, merchandise, and tie-ups are becoming increasingly important. Jaron Lanier (2011) has described the state of the music industry as leading to a form of "digital Maoism," wherein musicians are expected to earn a living from the sale of material goods such as T-shirts rather than their musical talents.[5]

To Lanier and others, this seems like a major shift, but it is not necessarily so in Japan—the second largest music market in the world (behind the United States)—where the CD remains a material token for value produced elsewhere. Physical formats accounted for only 30 percent of global music industry revenues in 2017, but they comprised 72 percent of Japan's.[6] While media convergence has destabilized media industries around the world and led to a growing concentration of media ownership, domestically, Japan's media companies were already concentrated to such a high degree that the impact of consolidation has been less apparent. Furthermore, in Japan, the music industry is organized around production companies (Marx 2012), which tend to prefer idols that perform multiple roles as singers, models, actors, and entertainers. In this system, many of the artists, or rather media performers, were never just musicians; they were always supposed to sell goods. While music sales have declined in Japan since 1998, the loss has not been as precipitous as in other parts of the world, because idols—appearing across multiple platforms and genres of performance, often simultaneously, as well as in person—cultivate greater intimacy with fan audiences, who are moved to make purchases. Like Japan's idol system, US labels are embracing "multiple rights" or "360 deals" as a new model for developing talent. In this arrangement, "artists share not just revenue from their album sales but concert, merchandise and other earnings with their label in exchange for more comprehensive career support."[7] This arrangement is not unlike what we see in Japan.

While the album has traditionally been the focus of the Japanese music industry, the AKB48 group flips this business model to make the single the primary product. With the development and spread of the digital CD from the 1990s,[8] the single CD typically included two tracks and a karaoke version of the title song. For AKB48, revenues from singles far outpace albums, which are still chart-toppers in their own right. Much as singles eclipse the album for idols, so has the idol music industry become ancillary to the larger economy of promotion, transmedia storytelling, and multimedia tie-ups. AKB48 takes this even further. With this group, the product is the affective experience of engaging idols across a multitude of not only media platforms but also face-to-face encounters. The music of AKB48 is produced as a means of patronage for fans, or a way to buy into interactions and relations and participate more intimately and intensively. Focusing on the birth and spread of the AKB48 model of "idols that you can meet," this book explores the tensions of affective economics in Japan today. Employing critical theory, we open the lessons of AKB48 to discussion beyond Japan. It turns out that there is a lot to that young man and his box of CDs, but to unpack it, we need to start at the beginning—way back in the 1970s, when a media-commodity system that included idols in the contemporary sense first took shape in Japan.

1 The Birth and Evolution of Idols in Japan

The year 1971 is often remembered as "the first year of the idol era" (*aidoru gannen*) (Kimura 2007: 260). That year, during the annual *Red and White Song Battle* (Kōhaku uta gassen), Japan's most watched television program, Minami Saori was introduced as a "teen idol" (*tiin no aidoru*). Not only did Minami sing hit songs such as "Seventeen" (*Jūnanasai*, 1971), but she also appeared frequently in the media; wherever she went, fans followed. For example, when Minami was featured on the cover of a weekly comics magazine, it marked not only cross-media promotion but also a convergence of readers, which increased sales (Okada 2008: 92). This points to a strategy called "media mix" (*media mikkusu*), which was established in Japan in the 1960s. It was not until the 1970s, however, that idols came to the fore of what Marc Steinberg calls Japan's "media-commodity system" (Steinberg 2012: 43). Importantly, this system generates desire for idols, who proliferate across media forms and become part of the everyday world. Simultaneously, the idol in the media mix is "a technology of attraction and diffusion" and "a technology of connection" (Steinberg 2012: 45).[1] Put somewhat differently, idols encourage intertextual and intimate media engagement across platforms, contexts, and venues (Galbraith and Karlin 2012).[2]

Also in 1971, idols came to be mass-produced on the television show *Birth of a Star!* (*Sutā tanjō*). A talent show where contestants performed for producers and a chance at the big time, *Birth of a Star!* suggested that anyone could be an idol. So it was that, in 1972, a thirteen-year-old Yamaguchi Momoe applied by postcard to be on the show. Although she finished second, Yamaguchi still debuted as a professional idol. Despite early struggles, Yamaguchi went on to a legendary career: she released thirty-two singles, including three number-one hits, and twenty-one albums; starred in fifteen feature films and several television dramas; and appeared on *Red and White Song Battle* for seven straight years. Indeed, such was Yamaguchi's popularity that her appearance in an advertising campaign for Pretz markedly increased sales of the snack food.

Following the rise of Yamaguchi, an entire industry sprang up to produce, promote, and profit from idols. By 1975, it was estimated that some seven hundred new idols had debuted in Japan (Okiyama 2007: 260) and people spoke of an "idol boom" (Aoyagi 2000: 316). The most successful of these new idols and emblematic of the boom was Pink Lady, a duo that appeared on *Birth of a Star!* in 1976 and went on to release nine number-one hits, five of which were consecutive million-selling singles; one single, "Chameleon Army" (*Kamereon āmii*, 1978), was on top of the charts for an astonishing sixty-three weeks. Pink Lady also became commercial pitchwomen for various products, ranging from children's books to ramen noodles, and practically everything they endorsed enjoyed a dramatic increase in sales.[3] The idol era was in full swing.

Known as the "golden age of idols" (*aidoru no ōgon jidai*), the 1980s were dominated by these transmedia and cross-genre performers, but none could surpass Matsuda Seiko, who debuted in 1980 and went on to have twenty-four consecutive number-one hits. As Yamaguchi Momoe had done with Pretz, Matsuda appeared and sang in a series of commercials for Pocky, which effectively raised the profile of the product, her songs, and herself. More than anyone before, Matsuda and her producers mastered the idol image, or the idol as image, which Matsuda—"Seiko-chan" to fans—performed and producers sold. In this way, Matsuda became an "image commodity" (Lukács 2010a: 24, 47) connecting companies, programs, products, and audiences. The circulation of the idol brought together producers and advertisers, content and commodities, audiences and consumers.

While idols declined in popularity at the end of the 1980s and into the early 1990s—the "idol ice age" (*aidoru hyōgaki*) or "winter period of idols" (*aidoru no fuyu no jidai*), often attributed to discontent with their artificiality (de Launey 1995: 209; Aoyagi 2000: 318; Ōtsuka 2004: 148)—things heated up again relatively quickly. Rocked by a devastating economic recession and difficulty transitioning to new paradigms, the 1990s has come to be known in Japan as "the lost decade" (*ushinawareta jūnen*).[4] Amid stagnation and anxiety, the achievements of the Japanese music and media industries were bright spots. "J-pop"—a term originating from the J-WAVE radio station in Tokyo, where it was used to refer to Japanese music that was played alongside the foreign music to which the station was dedicated—became attractive to young Japanese. The sound was not only "global" but also a global Japanese sound, which allowed fans to indulge in what Mōri Yoshitaka calls "the illusion of a globalized self" (Mōri 2009: 479). On the swell of J-pop, singers such as Utada Hikaru—whose music incorporated her impeccable English, her taste for American R&B, and world-class production techniques—enjoyed huge success. By the end of the 1990s, Utada's album *First Love* (1999) had sold 8.53 million copies in Japan (Mōri 2009: 476).

Even as J-pop rose, foreign music declined. In 1998, only ten albums of music by Western artists made the chart for the top hundred albums, and none were in the top ten (Mōri 2009: 476–77).[5] Writing at the time, Guy de Launey noted that musicians originating and operating outside of Japan had less of a presence in the Japanese market (de Launey 1995: 204). By his estimation, this had less to do with taste than marketing strategies that promoted Japanese musicians in Japan (de Launey 1995: 211–22). Among the factors that de Launey identified as contributing to the striking market dominance of Japanese music in the 1990s are television and tie-ups (de Launey 1995: 211–12, 218–19), which suggests the advantage of the media mix and its imperative to appear across media platforms and genres of performance.

What de Launey identified is the logic of idols, who in fact reached new heights of prominence in Japan in the late 1990s. Even as CD sales peaked in 1998 and began a steady decline, the male idol group SMAP enjoyed incredible success due to television appearances, tie-ups, and near-constant media exposure. One member in particular, Kimura Takuya, was a national heartthrob that appeared in a series of so-called trendy dramas (*torendi dorama*). Explaining the phenomenon of Kimura ("Kimutaku" to fans), Gabriella Lukács argues that transmedia and cross-genre deployment of idols establishes ties between media institutions and reinforces viewer commitments (Lukács 2010a: 31). Due to multiple and simultaneous appearances, idols become dense carriers of information and are read intertextually. Fans know and care more about their idols, which leads to a viewing experience that is "intimate" (Lukács 2010a: 30). The trendy drama adds to this by focusing not on story per se but rather on lifestyles, or the intertextual lives of idols and the characters they play, with tight production schedules resonating with the latest trends (Lukács 2010a: 40–44). All of this "makes participation in domestic media culture more pleasurable" (Lukács 2010a: 30). By placing idols at the heart of programming, Japanese broadcasters "succeeded not only in reviving a general interest in domestic televisual culture, but also in keeping transnational media out of the domestic market" (Lukács 2010a: 30). Japanese idol media thus dominated the domestic market. Trendy dramas such as *Beautiful Life* (Byūtifuru raifu, 2000), which stars Kimura Takuya, reached 41.3 percent of households in Japan (Lukács 2010b: 186).[6] In the 1990s, Fuji TV and TBS, the two major broadcasters associated with trendy dramas, produced more than 550 of them; a single three-month season could have seventeen or more airing at once (Lukács 2010a: 44). On the other hand, production of Japanese content in Japan for Japanese audiences made little room for foreign offerings; in the 1990s, Japanese broadcasters imported only 3 percent of their content (Lukács 2010a: 33).

Even as CD sales and ratings deteriorated, fans, who were motivated by their idols, could be counted on to tune in and make purchases. For this reason, idols became an increasingly important part of Japanese music and media markets at a time when they were facing the challenges of global competition and media convergence (Galbraith and Karlin 2016: 6–7). In a provocative turn of phrase, Lukács draws attention to how fans organize into "affective alliances" (Lukács 2010a: 54) around their idols.[7] To build on Lukács, affective alliances are not only between fans and idols, and between fans brought together by idols, but also between media producers, programs, and products brought together by idols in the Japanese domestic media market. As broadcasters and advertisers became increasingly dependent on them to attract viewers and buyers, SMAP and other male idols from the same production company leveraged "compounded star power" (Marx 2012: 43) to dominate Japanese television for decades.

Again, the affective dimensions of this are crucial. Like comparable acts such as the Backstreet Boys, SMAP consisted of five members with different styles and personalities that appealed to different fans.[8] In addition to standing for new forms of masculinity (Darling-Wolf 2004), the near-constant exposure of, and contact between, the members of SMAP fed into fan practices of reading into their "characters" and "relationships" (Karlin 2012; Nagaike 2012; Glasspool 2012). All of this can also be said of female idol groups with multiple members, which date back to media darlings such as Pink Lady and the Candies (Ōta 2011: 60–80; Okajima and Okada 2011: 50–61; Kitagawa 2013: 31–36). Beyond group members, intensive exposure across platforms and genres of performance lead to audiences knowing and caring more about idols, or intertextual and intimate engagement with their characters and stories, which can reinforce investments in idols and affective alliances with, against, and around them. In the late 1980s, for example, as tabloids and talk shows buzzed about her scandalous character and rumored relationship with Kondō Masahiko, viewers were compelled to side with or against Matsuda Seiko or her rival Nakamori Akina.

A separate but related development concerning affect is contact and communication with idols. Obviously, despite her cultivated image, not even Matsuda Seiko was ever just an image, as some critics might seem to suggest (Kijima 2012: 151–53). One need only review recordings of her appearances on television shows to confirm that members of the studio audience were responding wildly to her physical presence. This is even truer of concerts, which in Japanese industry and fan vernacular are referred to as "lives" (*raibu*), seeming to draw attention to the fact that things are occurring in "real time," a shared present. Indeed, the chants, dances, and so on among fans at idol concerts are a performance onto themselves. When fans number in the thousands, as at one of Matsuda's concerts, these performances become what Christine R. Yano refers to as "a spectacle of intimacy" (Yano 2004: 54). As with the idols that Yano examines, Matsuda wrote messages to her fans that appealed with saccharine self-performance and pleas for continued support (Aoyagi 2005: 185–93), which contributed to the explosive responses that she received at concerts. Be it SMAP or Matsuda Seiko, these rituals of relatively unmediated contact with fans are absolutely essential to affective alliances involving idols, which were intensified by the predecessors of AKB48 in the 1980s and 1990s.

2 The Democratization of Idols

During the golden age of idols in the mid-1980s and the idol revival in the late 1990s, the affective dimension of idols expanded with two female groups and the promise of greater audience participation. The first was Onyanko Club (aka "Pussycat Club"), which redefined the relationship between idols and fans. Onyanko Club was composed of fifty members selected from "ordinary schoolgirls" who appeared on Fuji Television's late show *All Night Fuji: High-School Girl Special* (Ōru naito Fuji: Joshi kōsei supesharu) in 1985. Given their own television show, *Sunset Meow Meow* (Yūyake nyan nyan), the members of Onyanko Club essentially just hung out, played games, and interacted with one another and the audience. At one level a show about nothing (Kinsella 1995: 235–36), *Sunset Meow Meow* was also a showcase for the young women, who appealed to the audience. They also regularly auditioned others to join them. The result was an ever-changing roster, as older members dropped out of the group and new ones were inducted in. Two things are significant about this formula: the ordinariness of members and the regular renewal of membership.

The members of Onyanko Club were "ordinary" (*futsū*) young women, which meant that they did not stand out as exceptionally beautiful or talented. If anything, many members were notably poor at singing, and being an idol came second to school obligations. As "ordinary schoolgirls," the idols of Onyanko Club were presented as "real" people, closer to the audience in life experiences than a star would be. This ordinariness made them approachable to fans.[1] The fact that they lacked extraordinary talent also leveled the playing field; one succeeded in Onyanko Club not by natural gifts but by hard work and perseverance (i.e., the spirit of *ganbaru*), which earned fan support. Fans shared in the idols' hardships and triumphs, laughed and cried with them, and idols appealed to fans by showcasing their personalities in interactions with other members. This was no less than an early form of reality television. Starting from an image as "amateur" (*shirōto*), the behind-the-scenes process of developing their individual characters was intentionally revealed to the audience, which positioned fans as "participating in the production of the idols" (Sakakura 2014: 37–38).

Also important was the regular "graduation" (*sotsugyō*) of members from the group and induction of new ones into it, which presented Onyanko Club as a showcase of idols that could be compared to others and were seeking support during a brief moment in the spotlight.[2] The Onyanko Club formula encouraged fans to organize around particular members; that many of these fans were adult men intensified the dynamic. So began the spirit of "supporting someone the most" (*dare wo ichi oshi suru*). The greater number of members, who were approachable in their ordinariness, vulnerable in their position, and in need of support, made Onyanko Club into something of a conglomeration of idol and fan groups in competition, which is fundamentally different from earlier idols.

Although active for only two years, in terms of sales, Onyanko Club was a phenomenal success. By the time the group disbanded in the fall of 1987, they had sold thirteen million copies of their singles, in addition to six million LPs; the market for "Onyanko goods" was valued at some ¥40 billion (Furuhashi 1989: 37). If we zero in on sales of singles, then we see that the secret to their success was a promotional strategy that brought idols and fans together and profited from the energy generated by their proximity. When Onyanko Club released a new single, they would go on a promotional tour of event spaces across Japan, which served to connect them to local fans and contributed to a festival-like atmosphere. This contact was literal, in not only the sense that the spaces where they performed were small and fans were close to the stage, but also in that if fans bought a copy of the single, they would be allowed to shake hands with members. Like politicians campaigning for support, Onyanko Club idols connected with and excited their base, which contributed to soaring sales. As Furuhashi Kenji argues, the national tours of small venues and handshaking events were a turning point:

> What this did was take idols, who until that point were seen on television or from a distance in a concert hall, and turn them into an existence that could be seen up close on stages on the rooftops of department stores, where we could take pictures with our own cameras, shake their hands, and even exchange a few words. In this way, the distance between idols and fans (maniacs) was reduced to almost nothing. (Furuhashi 1989: 37)

This closing of distance, or bringing idols and fans into closer proximity, is a key development in the idol system leading to AKB48. Rather than being a fan looking at a photograph in a magazine or a recorded appearance on television, or being at a concert with thousands of others and seeing the idol only on the big screen projection or distant stage, the idol was now literally within reach. The renewed investment and interest in idols, and competition between them and between their fans, led to Onyanko Club concerts or "lives" being some of the most lively the industry had ever seen.

Throughout, the audience was introduced to the production process of the idol, or the "reality" behind the image, which is also true of the second of the two transformative idol groups, Morning Musume (aka "Morning Girls"). If the members of Onyanko Club were selected from among "ordinary schoolgirls," then the original members of Morning Musume were a group of failed vocalists. On the television show and talent search *Asayan* in 1997, the singer Tsunku was auditioning young women to be the new vocalist for his band Sharam Q, but instead found himself intrigued by five of the runners up (Macias and Machiyama 2004: 55). These young women were issued a challenge to sell 50,000 copies of their demo single in just five days of promotional events (Sakakura 2014: 46). Approaching people on the street and generating word of mouth through various means of engagement with audiences, the young women managed to sell the required number of copies in four days spread out over the month of November. Thoroughly impressed, and using the compelling origin story of these underdogs and grassroots momentum of their supporters (Sakakura 2014: 39), Tsunku officially debuted the five women as Morning Musume.

There are a number of important aspects of this story, which of course fed back into the media-commodity system, but two are especially germane to the discussion at hand. First, from television, where they technically failed as vocalists, the original members of Morning Musume hit the streets to redeem themselves by selling CDs. They did this by appealing directly to fans for support, which marks their transition from would-be vocalists to an idol group. That is, their interactions with fans and appeal for support are at the core of the story, as opposed to, for example, the quality of the music and how it drew fans to them, which one might expect to see in the story of an indies band. Second, this fan base then followed them and infused an Onyanko Club level of energy into their concerts, which might be considered a continuation of their grassroots appeal alongside their successful mainstream media career over the following decade. While the mainstream audience included the demographic of young girls who might look up to idols as "role models" (Aoyagi 2005: 56), the grassroots audience notably included older men (Macias and Machiyama 2004: 56–57). For his part, Tsunku (2000: 98–100) admits to courting an audience of men—weakened by economic and social upheaval in the 1990s—with the image of "small and unthreatening girls." Separate from these aspects of Morning Musume, its fluctuating lineup, which shrank and expanded with regular graduations and auditions, was also important.[3] This kept things fresh and new, and though it never reached the sheer number of Onyanko Club, the group did grow to include over a dozen members at a time, who competed for fans and the spotlight. In all of this, the major lesson, as Sakakura underscores, was that success could be achieved by harnessing "the participation of fans" (Sakakura 2014: 44). This is where AKB48, the second coming of Onyanko Club, would eclipse Morning Musume in the 2000s.

3 "Idols That You Can Meet"

Every day in Japan, numerous idols are performing. Of these, only a minority appears in the mass media, while the rest operate as "underground" (*chika*), "street" (*rojō*), "net" (*netto*), or "indies" (*indiizu*) idols with sometimes only a handful of highly dedicated fans. While an analysis of production logic does much to explain idols in the context of an integrated system of media and commodities in Japan, it cannot account for these other idols, and herein lies an important point: Perhaps even more than a type of media performer, idols are fundamentally performers that appeal directly to fans for support. Intimate interactions with fans are characteristic of idols, whose existence depends on cultivating and maintaining relationships with fans. This is why Kyary Pamyu Pamyu, a cutesy female artist who may superficially appear to be an idol, denies that designation: "In my opinion, the job of an idol is more or less to suck up to men, like thinking about what they can do to catch male fans' attention."[1] The dynamic is not necessarily limited to capturing male fans' attention, as male idols such as SMAP and others from their production company appeal directly to female fans with the goal of winning their hearts. Regardless of gender, idols are meant to be objects of affection. The relationship between idols and fans can be experienced as friendship, even love, and cultivating it is key to an idol's success.

Rather than a media phenomenon, AKB48 started out as idols who performed live for small audiences and appealed directly to fans in the Akihabara area of Tokyo. This emphasis on the live experience of copresence with idols in a small, intimate venue was something of a departure for the group's producer, Akimoto Yasushi, who was also the mastermind behind Onyanko Club in the 1980s. In Akihabara in the early 2000s, Akimoto saw the emergence of maid cafés—establishments where young women dressed in character costumes and served a clientele that included dedicated regulars—as a sign of the evolution of Japanese consumer sensibilities. To facilitate such interactions and relations, Akimoto conceived of a group of idols appearing in an intimate venue with tickets costing only a fraction of other concerts or theater performances (Akimoto and Tahara 2013: 19–21).[2] The fact that Akimoto found inspiration in maid cafés and located the planned venue in Akihabara suggests that the initial intended audience for AKB48 was men, who were the overwhelming majority of regulars at maid cafés and people in Akihabara at the time (Morikawa 2003: 6–7). In its early years, AKB48's core fans were indeed men, and this gendered dynamic continues to be crucial to the affective economics of the group.

Given its current dominant status in terms of media appearances and CD sales, some might be surprised to hear that AKB48 was not an immediate hit. Those who witnessed the group's formation in Akihabara recall receiving fliers printed out on simple copy paper, which was for them nothing if not "suspicious" (*ayashii*).[3] Most must have opted to keep their distance, because according to Akimoto, AKB48's debut performance attracted an audience of only seven people.[4] Nevertheless, AKB48 did eventually find its footing and reach the initially planned forty-eight members—just slightly fewer than Onyanko Club, but not always or necessarily appearing together as a large group.[5] Instead, the members were divided into three teams on a rotating schedule, so that one team performed live at the AKB48 Theater in Akihabara almost every day year-round. AKB48's slogan, "idols that you can meet" (*ai ni ikeru aidoru*), speaks to their appeal to an audience that wants to see idols in person regularly.

The space where fans come to meet their idols, the AKB48 Theater, is a peculiar one. It is located above the discount chain store Don Quijote in the central part of Akihabara along its main thoroughfare, Chūō Street. Situated on the eighth floor, its defining characteristic is that it is "very small" (Hamano 2012: 90). The theater seats only 145 people and can accommodate a maximum of 250 people. The space occupied by the AKB48 Theater was not designed to house a live venue. As evidence of this, the AKB48 Theater has at its center, in the middle of audience seating, two massive support pillars for the building, which block some of the audience's view of the stage. Despite these limitations, the architecture of the AKB48 Theater has contributed to the formation of fan audiences, in that only a small number of people at a time can see a live show; when one does get in, the audience is very close to the stage, a mere two meters from it in the front row. In sum, the theater is an intimate space that ensures a powerful feeling of copresence.

As Hamano Satoshi—a researcher that became interested in the phenomenon of AKB48 and conducted auto-ethnographic fieldwork on his journey into fandom—points out, the two pillars in the AKB48 Theater not only block some of the audience's view, but also encourage audience members to focus on the idols appearing in their limited lines of sight (Hamano 2012: 124–32). The idols respond to this limitation by circulating around the stage to ensure that they are visible to all members of the audience, even if only briefly. Although originally skeptical about the appeal of AKB48 and finding the group's fans to be "somewhat pathetic," Hamano recounts an experience of being deeply affected by a moment when he recognized an idol on stage—and she seemed to recognize him back (Hamano 2015). This feeling of "recognition" (*shōnin*), of eyes meeting, was something akin to "love at first sight" (*hitomebore*). As Hamano understands it, the AKB48 Theater is "a platform for face-to-face communication," where fans can "savor an illusory experience that is close to 'the unexpected moment when our eyes met'" (Hamano 2012: 89, 132). The initially skeptical Hamano could not deny the powerfully moving experience of interacting with an idol, which was for him not unlike a religious experience, and he converted into a devoted fan of AKB48 (Hamano 2015). If we resist the urge to dismiss fans and instead take them seriously, then an experience such as Hamano's is neither self-delusion nor a suspension of disbelief, but in fact real "relationality" (Hamano 2012: 164). At the AKB48 Theater, one falls in love with idols by design, but this is nonetheless still love.

In 2006, AKB48 released its third single, "I Wanted to See You" (*Aitakatta*), which became a signature number performed at the start of live shows at the AKB48 Theater. The song begins with the phrase, "I wanted to see you," repeated three times with enthusiasm, punctuated by an English "yes," shouted by all the performers and audience members in unison; these four lines are repeated and then followed by "You..." When saying these lines, the idols look at members of the audience and seem to be speaking to them, and the audience returns the words and gaze. At times, the idols and audience, who are in close proximity, make eye contact and wave to one another. When the members of AKB48 sing "You...," which in Japanese is a second-person pronoun (*kimi*) followed by a particle indicating direction (*ni*), they draw out the sound of the particle and double the indication of direction by pointing directly at members of the audience, who often reciprocate the gesture. Given their close proximity, members of AKB48 and the audience often recognize who is pointing at whom. After the show, when the idols used to give members of the audience high fives (a charged moment of physical contact), one might mention to her fan, "We made eye contact back there." It is hard not to see this as a form of flirtation, which the idol does to earn support, or to encourage fans to fall and stay in love.

Indeed, fans recognize themselves as supporters of idols. The member of AKB48 that a fan points to—the one that he wants to see and be seen by—is known as "the member I support" (*oshimen*). The fan not only buys merchandise and photographic prints featuring his idol, but also makes a point of shouting her name when she appears on stage and sings. The music written for AKB48, as is common for idols, makes sure that popular members get to sing small parts on their own or as duets, which provides an opportunity for fans to shout the idol's name and show support (for her, not another idol, which is registered by members on stage, as well as the audience).[6] "Talk" (*tōku*), which refers to times where idols banter on stage instead of singing, are important chances for the audience to know them better and shout out responses in conversations—Hamano's "face-to-face communication"—that are both private and public, personal and shared, constructed and real. There are apparently no scripts for such "talk," which is relatively free-form, and the idols use the space to express themselves in a less-filtered way (Sakakura 2014: 41).

The foundation of AKB48 was built on shrinking the distance between fans and idols, who become real people that fans can meet and interact with regularly. The fundamental principle of the AKB48 Theater, where "the distance between idols and fans (maniacs) is reduced to almost nothing" (Furuhashi 1989: 37), and indeed, of AKB48 as "idols that you can meet," is the engineering of affective encounters. This tactic carried over from Onyanko Club, which should not be too surprising, given that Akimoto produced both groups. However, from Onyanko Club to AKB48, the direction was reversed: Rather than going from the media to the stage where they can meet fans as Onyanko Club did, AKB48 went from the stage to the media. This reversal is vital—something like the grassroots fan-building exercise of Morning Musume, but radically extended to four years rather than limited to just four days on the street and shaking hands. These four years, between their debut in the theater in Akihabara in 2005 and mainstream media breakout in 2009, are when the affective core of AKB48 was forged in interactions and relations with mostly male fans. In short, AKB48 focused on developing affective relations between idols and fans, which then drove sales and the group's reach to a wider audience.

4 The Affective Economics of the Idol Industry

In many ways, AKB48 can be understood in terms of affective economics. Jenkins (2006: 73), for example, draws attention to "inspirational consumers" or "loyalists," who constitute only a small percentage of the audience, but make up a disproportionate amount of purchases. Part of affective economics is attracting loyalists, invigorating them, and harnessing the power of their activity. While Jenkins is primarily considering brands and advertising in North America, there is much here that resonates with idols in Japan (Karlin 2012: 85–86; also Lukács 2010a). However, by shifting the discussion from brands to idols, we can begin to account more thoroughly for the missing aspect of labor, specifically the labor that idols do to attract and invigorate loyalists, whose power of activity can be harnessed.

In an article based on interactions with "net idols" (*netto aidoru*) in Japan, Gabriella Lukács underscores the enormous amount of effort that goes into being attractive to fans, which she calls "the labor of cute" (Lukács 2015: 487, 496).[1] Idols labor to be cute, or *kawaii* in Japanese, a word that combines *kanji* (modified Chinese logographs) meaning "possible" (*ka*) and "love" (*ai*). To be cute is to be "lovable" (Madge 1998: 157), and idols labor to be so. Since cuteness became a media and consumer-culture phenomenon in Japan in the 1970s, idols, who not coincidentally first appeared in that same decade, have become role models for many girls and women (Kinsella 1995: 225–37). In his ethnography of idol culture in Japan, Aoyagi Hiroshi suggests that the symbolic function of an idol is to successfully navigate social maturation and develop a persona that is "publicly adorable" (Aoyagi 2005: 63). Idols are introduced in magazines and on television as ideals for the youth of their time. They are also carriers of information about lifestyle and fashion for people more generally (Lukács 2010a: 29–31, 43, 51–52). As models, singers, dancers, personalities, and actors/actresses, idols also embody the ideal of a creative, communicative subject that works well with others and gains their love and support, an ideal that began to rise in many postindustrial nations in the 1970s (Lazzarato 1996: 133–37) and further took hold in Japan in the economic recession and rise of flexible employment in the 1990s (Allison 2009: 90–91). AKB48 intensifies this model of laboring to be cute or lovable in interactions with other idols and fans, which is also an ongoing struggle to maintain a publicly adorable personality.

As Lukács rightly points out, this is a form of labor, specifically affective labor.[2] In philosophy, affect refers to a modification or variation produced in a body in interaction with another body, which increases or diminishes the body's power of activity. In his critique of classic Marxism, Antonio Negri connects affect to "the power to act" and "value from below," which precedes and exceeds the relations of capital (Negri 1999: 78–79). In later work with Michael Hardt, however, Negri identifies "affective labor," which "produces or manipulates affects" (Hardt and Negri 2004: 108). Certainly this is an apt description of what idols do: generating "a feeling of ease, well-being, satisfaction, excitement, passion—even a sense of connectedness or community" (Hardt 1999: 96). Furthermore, idols mobilize fans, who are in many ways also ideal laborers of the new regime: active, productive, social, communicative, and networked (Lazzarato 1996: 142). If, as Maurizio Lazzarato argues, the corporation profits to the extent that it has "the capacity to activate and manage productive cooperation" (Lazzarato 1996: 134), then it does so through the deployment of idols. To put this somewhat differently, idols are the key to activating and managing productive cooperation among fans, as can be observed in shared movements in relation to idols.

In numerous publications (e.g., Tanaka 2010; Ōta 2011; Kitagawa 2013), the commercial success of AKB48 is tied to the intense devotion of its fans. AKB48's success depends on capitalizing on relations between idols and fans, techniques that are collectively referred to as the "AKB business model" (*AKB shōhō*). Entire books have been written to explain it (e.g., Sayawaka 2013), but the AKB business model can simply be understood as tying access, participation, and fan activity to CD sales. As Sakakura succinctly summarizes it, the revolutionary model is that "direct contact and concerts are the linchpin in CD sales, direct experiences are the main content, and CDs and songs serve as tools for them" (Sakakura 2014: 30). To repeat and rephrase somewhat to underscore the point, the main content is not the music, but the direct experience, which can be accessed with the purchase of a CD.

This is accomplished by packaging CDs with "premiums" (*omake*), for example, tickets to events where fans can interact with idols more intimately. Historically, premiums have been an important part of the media mix, or media-commodity system that ties character images to products, but the AKB business model marks a significant shift. Looking back to an early example of media mix, Marc Steinberg (2012: 37–86) shows how the Meiji Seika confectionary company encouraged consumption of Marble Chocolates by linking the purchase to stickers of the characters of *Astro Boy* (Tetsuwan Atomu, 1963–1966). The character-image stickers were the premium. In the case of AKB48, the purchase of a CD is rewarded with tickets to special events such as "handshake events" (*akushukai*) (Figures 1 and 2). The experience is the premium. This practice was already anticipated by Onyanko Club and other idols in earlier decades, but AKB48 has done more than any other group to systematize the relationship between CD and premium-experience, or purchasing material objects for opportunities for copresence and connection.

Given that seeing the idols and being seen by them is a central tenet of AKB48, it should come as no surprise that handshake events proved to be extremely popular with fans. Not only does the fan get to meet his idol, but also touch her hand and exchange a personal greeting, entertaining the fantasy that she recognizes (if not also loves) him from multiple previous encounters (Hamano 2012: 79–88). Even after buying a CD and getting a ticket to a handshake event, fans, who show up in droves, have to wait in line to reach their idol, with whom they interact one-on-one for only a few precious moments. There are books written by and for fans outlining strategies on how to use this time most effectively. Ultimately, even if fans do not want a copy of an AKB48 CD, they still buy it for the premium, if not also to show support. This leads to AKB48 fans owning many physical copies of CDs, even multiple copies of the same CD, all purchased when first released and at full retail

Figures 1 and 2 *From images to affects: Character stickers of Astro Boy included as a premium with the purchase of Meiji Seika's Marble Chocolates from 1963 (top) have evolved today to include tickets to an AKB48 handshake event included with this purchase of the group's twelfth single CD "Namida Surprise!" released in 2009 (bottom).*

Source: kumajiroupapa, "ALWAYS sanchōme no yūhi '64 koraborēshon shōhin 'Tetsuwan Atomu Māburuchokorēto,'" *Kumajī Ōkoku no Kumajirō*, March 17, 2012, http://blog.livedoor.jp/kumajiroupapa/archives/52002737.html.

price to synchronize with the tie-up event, which is somewhat anachronistic in a world moving toward digital downloads and streaming music services.

After spending four years doing primarily local performances in its small theater in Akihabara, AKB48 had developed a devoted fan base of followers and supporters. Before changing to a more exclusive system, one could buy a ticket for a show by just lining up on the street in front of Don Quijote, which resulted in hundreds of fans gathering ever earlier in the morning to get ahead of others and try for a ticket. Although AKB48 was marketed as "idols that you can meet," this slogan was not true for many fans. Hence the increasingly long lines at handshake events, where direct contact was still possible (with premium purchase). If one could not see them in the intimate setting of the theater, then they could at least see them for a few moments one-on-one, touch their hand, and look into their eyes.

Frustrations were exacerbated by AKB48's massive break into the mainstream media from 2009, when seemingly overnight the idols began to appear much more prominently and regularly in print and broadcast media, as well as in advertising. Naturally, success here pulled them away from the theater, the physical place of Akihabara and time interacting with fans there. Many fans felt left behind, unseen and unheard, and alienated. It would not be too much to call this a crisis moment, given that the essential dynamic was in question. But Akimoto Yasushi found a novel solution in the form of structured idol-fan interaction, participatory coproduction of the group beyond the theater, and a franchise-like model of similar theaters and sister groups across Japan and abroad.

5 The General Election

As the story goes, Akimoto Yasushi overheard fans in the AKB48 Theater complaining that the composition of the group did not reflect their desires.[1] Composition here means which idols are positioned most prominently on stage, get the most exposure, and are highlighted with solos, duets, and so on. One might assume that this would be determined by who is the most attractive or talented in the group, but such was not the case. This was not, however, in and of itself the problem. Fans understood the composition of the group to be the result of a popularity contest, but were complaining that their input was not a part of deciding the contest. Specifically, many believed that Akimoto was unfairly pushing Maeda Atsuko, who was taken to be his personal favorite. This was indeed a serious issue, because much of the appeal of AKB48 was the expectation that fan participation directly influenced the composition and activities of the group (Sakakura 2014: 48).

Rather than deny that the composition of AKB48 was more or less decided through a popularity contest, Akimoto embraced it with the General Election (*sōsenkyō*). Not only responding to fan criticism but also building on the concept of "the member I support," Akimoto told fans to step up and decide for themselves who would become AKB48's "center" (*sentā*), or the most popular member who enjoys the most exposure, and the "select members" (*senbatsu membā*) around her.[2] Fans vote in the General Election to determine these positions, or simply vote for the member they support, regardless of rank. The members of AKB48 who are voted into the select group then sing the next single and appear in its promotional video. This enfranchisement encourages fans to participate in the General Election and to have an impact on the career of the member they support, as well as the overall composition of AKB48.

While a General Election sounds very democratic, fans need to buy new copies of a designated CD that comes packaged with a ballot in order to vote. That is, the ballot is the premium. There is no limit to how many votes can be cast by an individual, who can simply buy more CDs to get more ballots. Even more so than tickets to handshake events, this use of the premium spurs AKB48 fans to buy multiple copies of the same CD, leading to record-breaking sales. This is further intensified by outright competition between fans and members of AKB48, whose numbers ballooned from 48 to over 159, and beyond the initial group to include members of its sister groups in other areas, as many as 398 (as of January 2019).[3]

In 2009, when the General Election was first held, AKB48 was not in the top ten of the Oricon Yearly Singles Chart. Instead, the chart was dominated by the male idol successors of SMAP, namely Arashi, KAT-TUN, and Kanjani 8. However, in 2010, with the General Election established and AKB48 gaining more media exposure, they had the top two spots with "Beginner" (954,283 copies sold) and "Heavy Rotation" (713,275 copies sold).[4] The increase in sales correlated with greater participation in the General Election (Table 1), when a rivalry between AKB48 members Maeda Atsuko and Ōshima Yūko mobilized fans to buy CDs and vote. Indeed, in addition to more people buying more CDs to cast more votes for more members (a distributed increase), a major factor in AKB48's increased sales was Ōshima's fans (a focused increase), who

Table 1 *AKB48 General Election: Votes cast*

#	Votes
1st	NA
2nd	377,786
3rd	1,166,145
4th	1,384,122
5th	2,646,847
6th	2,689,427
7th	3,287,736
8th	3,255,400
9th	3,382,368
10th	3,836,652

Source: Oricon

voted her into the center position over Maeda, the winner of the first election in 2009 and the recognized center of AKB48 (Table 2). In 2009, Maeda earned 4,630 votes, but in 2010, Ōshima earned 31,448. In 2011, when Maeda's fans mobilized to support her comeback, she earned 139,892 votes out of a total 1,081,392 cast for the top 40 spots.[5] The AKB business model, which mobilized fans to buy CDs in order to participate, proved to be extremely effective: In 2011, AKB48 had *all top five spots* on the Oricon Yearly Singles Chart, a record achievement that they repeated in 2012. That year, each of their top five singles sold over a million copies. Furthermore, AKB48's sister group SKE48 (from Nagoya) held spots eight through ten, leaving only six and seven open for the male idol group Arashi.

AKB48

Table 2 *AKB48 General Election: Single CD sales*

#	Year	Single Release	Single Song	CD Sales
1st	2009	AKB48 13th Single	言い訳Maybe (Iiwake Maybe)	145,776
2nd	2010	AKB48 17th Single	ヘビーローテーション (Heavy Rotation)	881,519
3rd	2011	AKB48 22nd Single	フライングゲット (Flying Get)	1,625,849
4th	2012	AKB48 27th Single	ギンガムチェック (Gingham Check)	1,316,240
5th	2013	AKB48 32nd Single	恋するフォーチュンクッキー (Koi Suru Fortune Cookie)	1,549,343
6th	2014	AKB48 37th Single	心のプラカード (Koi no Placard)	1,061,976
7th	2015	AKB48 41st Single	ハロウィン・ナイト (Halloween Night)	1,331,573
8th	2016	AKB48 45th Single	LOVE TRIP/しあわせを分けなさい (Love Trip/Shiawase wo Wakenasai)	1,217,750
9th	2017	AKB48 49th Single	#好きなんだ (Sukinanda)	1,129,165
10th	2018	AKB48 52nd Single	Teacher Teacher	1,820,963

Source: Oricon

The General Election marks a significant recognition of fans' affection, attachments, and activities as a source of value. Faced with public scrutiny over apparent manipulation of fans and encouragement of wasteful consumption, Ōshima explained to her critics that, "Votes are love" (*tōhyō wa mina-san no ai*).[6] If votes are love, then fans who love their idols more will buy more CDs in order to vote more times and express that love. In turn, idols labor to earn the love of fans. When Ōshima was voted into the center position, she led AKB48 in singing their smash single "Heavy Rotation" (*Hebii rōtēshon*, 2010), which begins with these words: "I want you! (I want you!) I need you! (I need you!) I love you! (I love you!)" In the context of the General Election, it almost seemed like Ōshima, the new center, was saying the words to her supporters, who joined the members of AKB48 in echoing them back to her.[7]

While acknowledging that one buys votes in the General Election, note that it is the electorate, not the candidates, who do the buying, motivated by love. Idols inspire their fans to act as supporters, or, put another way, to act on their love. What might you think if you discovered hundreds of AKB48 CD singles emptied of their ballots and discarded in a trash heap? Perhaps that it is a waste of money and resources. But what might the fan who bought those CDs think? Perhaps that it was a meaningful and fulfilling way to support his idol and express his love by participating in the General Election. Fans who buy dozens of copies of the same CD are not ashamed of their actions—quite the opposite, actually. AKB48 fans sometimes pile their CD purchases up, take photographs, and post them to social media. When a fan posts a photograph like this, it is with the expectation that fellow fans—and indeed the idols, who are also online interacting (and maintaining relationships) with fans—will see it and perhaps comment. The expectation is that the fan's actions, his labor of love, will be recognized. In the process, the relationship and its value are also recognized. Fellow fans and idols recognize and evaluate the bulk CD purchase as an expression of love, or by a metric other than an economic understanding of value.

Consider the following scenarios. Angered by a scandal that saw their idol banished from Tokyo to a sister group (HKT48 in Fukuoka) in 2012 and determined to right the wrong, fans rallied to elect Sashihara Rino to AKB48's center position in the General Election in 2013. Famous for her rapport with fans and use of social media to interact with them, Sashihara received a record 150,570 votes, with one of her fans claiming to have spent approximately fourteen million yen to buy 9,108 votes for her.[8] The incredible result was that Sashihara bounced back from a scandal (not common for idols, especially when they are young women [West 2006: 242–83]) and reached the pinnacle of AKB48—the first time someone from a sister group held the coveted center position. Fans were happy, because they achieved their goal and kept Sashihara in the spotlight. And Akimoto Yasushi, who had banished Sashihara and angered the fans, smiled all the way to the bank.

But it did not end there. In the General Election in 2014, a forty-two-year-old strawberry farmer, who claims to spend between eight and nine million yen a year to support his idol, bought 4,600 CDs to vote for Sashihara, only to see her come in second place.[9] While in some ways the strawberry farmer failed, he succeeded in expressing his love for Sashihara and having it recognized by others. The election results also provided a reason for fans to rally behind Sashihara in 2015.

Another remarkable story from the General Election in 2014 was Takahashi Juri, a young member of AKB48 who for two years had failed to break into the top 48 spots (i.e., a lower bracket of select members). Deciding it was time to vote her up in rank, one of Takahashi's fans spent ¥31,502,400 to buy CDs and votes for her; although the supporter chose to remain anonymous, he took and posted pictures to prove the enormity of his investment.[10] Perhaps the reader thinks that these fans of Sashihara and Takahashi are fools, but they could respond that people do foolish things when in love (and hence evaluate their actions positively).

If the "affect" in affective economics can be understood as the "power to act" and "value from below" (Negri 1999: 78–79), then a critic might suggest that the AKB business model generally and the General Election specifically demonstrate how it is captured in, for example, the practice of getting fans to buy multiple copies of the same CD to support their idols. Struck by the sight of young men purchasing multiple copies of the same CD single, comedian Okamura Takashi slammed AKB48 for its exploitative business practices.[11] Drawing a comparison to "host clubs," where professional male entertainers sell female clients the fantasy of a romantic relationship and encourage them to order overpriced food and drink to boost their monthly sales and rank in the club (Takeyama 2005: 207–208), Okamura described AKB48 as a "reverse host club" (*gyaku hosuto kurabu*). In this statement, Okamura plays on the widespread perception that women are manipulated and taken advantage of in host clubs. In calling the dynamic a reverse host club, Okamura suggests that AKB48 idols are like hosts selling the fantasy of a romantic relationship, which they abuse to take advantage of male fans, who are in the same position as hosts' female clients. Worse still, he says, is that all they get is a handshake and smile.

While Okamura is right to highlight the similarities between hosts and idols engaged in intimate relations with clients and fans and encouraging them to make purchases in order to boost their rank, he falls into a familiar trap by reducing this to a narrative of exploitation. A critique of affective economics requires a more nuanced approach, which comes from closer examination. For example, Akiko Takeyama, who conducted fieldwork in Tokyo host clubs, does not see clients as purely victims or hosts as victimizers—or the other way around, hosts as purely victims of employers and clients that (ab)use them for their own purposes. Instead, Takeyama argues that the host club, like affective economics more generally, "satisfies multiple players and institutions in mutual yet asymmetrical ways" (Takeyama 2010: 238). Takeyama points out that Japan's affect economy is "nested in the service and entertainment industry" (Takeyama 2010: 238), which invites an application of her analysis of hosts (service) to the case of idols (entertainment industry). As Takeyama suggests of hosts, an asymmetrical relationship is also characteristic of relations between idols and fans (Yano 2004: 47), but this is not to say that these relationships are not real or meaningful for those involved (Ho 2012a: 177–179). Furthermore, insofar as affective labor can be deeply rewarding (Lukács 2013: 48), neither idols nor fans—all engaged in forms of affective labor, laboring for love in relation to one another—are purely victims. That said, however, it is necessary to account for other players and institutions that set up and profit from these relations. We need, that is, to consider the political economy of idols.

6 Toward a Critical Political Economy of Idols

While recognizing that fans are active agents and producers of value, identity, and meaning, it seems not only insufficient but also irresponsible to avoid talking about the structures that enable, limit, and profit from active fans, especially when they are as blatant as in the case of AKB48. This is a difficult challenge, however, when critical approaches are taken to be critiques of fans or media or popular culture, tout court. We find ourselves at odds with a new orthodoxy that celebrates choice and pleasure, which, as David Graeber underscores, aligns scholarship with "the very ideology of the new global market" (Graeber 2004: 100–101).

The problem is, we think, a deep-seated one, at least in the North American context and probably beyond. In its formative early years in North America, scholarship on fandom positioned itself against critiques of consumers as passive or manipulated by producers. For example, in contributions to *The Adoring Audience*, John Fiske, a scholar of television, argues that fans are not just consumers but also producers (Fiske 1992: 37–41), and Lawrence Grossberg, a representative of American cultural studies, shows how meaning is made out of given media forms, even as fans invest affectively in them (Grossberg 1992: 52–57). Perhaps most representative of this position is

Henry Jenkins, who argues in his foundational work *Textual Poachers* that fans are active producers of not only meaning but also other texts, including fanzine stories and novels, art prints, songs, videos, and performances (Jenkins 1992: 46). This understanding of the active agency of consumers is the legacy of audience studies, reception theory, and British cultural studies, which are sometimes brought together under the banner of the Birmingham School.[1] This school of thought is then contrasted with the Marxist-inspired critique of mass culture of the Frankfurt School.

The Frankfurt School refers to a school of social theory and philosophy founded in the interwar period and associated with the Institute for Social Research at the Goethe University Frankfurt. Its members were dissidents that did not feel at home in the capitalist, fascist, and communist systems sweeping Europe. Chief among their contributions was work by Max Horkheimer and Theodor Adorno on the topic of "the culture industry."[2] Referring to a loose grouping of corporations, the culture industry produces mass culture, or media and material culture for mass consumption. It does this in pursuit of profit. If forms are profitable, they are produced, and produced again and again. The resultant "sameness" (Horkheimer and Adorno 2002: 94), which can be understood as standardization characteristic of the logic of mass production, is masked by pseudo-individuation. For example, hit songs have very similar structures, but are differentiated by hooks and frills.[3] This means that consumers essentially get the same thing over and over in a circuit of mass production and consumption. While nothing if not rational for the culture industry in its pursuit of profit, as Horkheimer and Adorno see it, such rationalization leads not to liberation of consciousness and "enlightenment," but rather a fettering of consciousness in a system that is dumbing and numbing (Horkheimer and Adorno 2002: 97).

The power of the culture industry lies in its ability to produce a passive and dependent consuming public. The "prepared" consumer is rewarded by repetition, which they come to expect and demand in predictable pleasures (Horkheimer and Adorno 2002: 98–99). As Horkheimer and Adorno put it, "The products of the culture industry are such that they can be alertly consumed in a state of distraction" (Horkheimer and Adorno 2002: 100). The culture industry keeps the consuming public in a state of distraction, which is to say that it occupies minds. Pleasure-seeking becomes routine, even as work and leisure come to resemble one another as routine. In this Marxist-inspired critique, mass consumption and pleasure reproduce workers in the system of mass production. In this way, Horkheimer and Adorno argue, "Entertainment is the prolongation of work under late capitalism" (Horkheimer and Adorno 2002: 109). With limited time and relentless stress to manage, what comes easily is taken with ease. The result, by Horkheimer and Adorno's estimation, is that workers are hemmed into the system "so tightly, body and soul, that they unresistingly succumb to whatever is proffered to them" (Horkheimer and Adorno 2002: 106). Ultimately, Horkheimer and Adorno write, "The power of the culture industry lies in its unity with fabricated need" (Horkheimer and Adorno 2002: 109), or in fabricating and satisfying needs in mass, which subjugates people to "the total power of capital" (Horkheimer and Adorno 2002: 94).

Critiques of this approach to the culture industry are numerous and varied. Some accuse the Frankfurt School generally and Adorno specifically of being an elitist, sexist, classist, traditionalist, and many other "-ists" besides (Modleski 1986: 156). Others draw attention to the problematic conflation of forms of media and material culture. Surely a mass-produced song is not the same as a mass-produced car, and they must be evaluated differently, which is to say textually versus functionally (Gendron 1986: 32). The most helpful critiques focus on what appears to be the suggestion of a static, ahistorical system (Smythe 1981: 268–71), which cannot account for change. Rather than a standardized commodity produced for and pushed onto the masses, popular music, for example, has changed with the times. Not every manufactured star or hit becomes a star or a hit, which implies that the support of the masses must be won, even if mass circulation and repetition can win consumers over to a certain extent.[4] This in turn suggests that producers must be responsive to the demands of consumers, and consumption is productive in providing feedback, which has been noted of capitalism since the 1970s (Lazzarato 1996: 140–43).

While the culture industry approach encounters trouble in accounting for individual agency, active audiences, and more complex dynamics of power, the insights of the Frankfurt School are not entirely unhelpful in understanding contemporary media and material culture. Read generously, Horkheimer and Adorno point us in the direction of critically assessing the system of "free choice and pleasure," but they do not anticipate the forms that would emerge in affective economics. With this in mind, we can say that, as developed in Japan in the 1970s, idols are products of the culture industry. W. David Marx argues that idols appear with the frequency that they do in Japan because producers seek "stable profits within the Japanese entertainment industry," and they seek profits "over creative works (the culture itself)" (Marx 2012: 51). In a simple example, advertisement deals are the most lucrative for producers, so they prefer performers that are "publicly adorable"—idols—and that can secure those deals rather than anyone controversial or threatening, to say nothing of their talents as an artist, which matter very little. Although Horkheimer and Adorno did not write about Japan specifically, such a critique might well have come from the Frankfurt School. For his part, however, Marx (2012: 52) draws attention to the need to discuss the "missing factor" of the audience, which an analysis of AKB48 brings to light.

Now, standardization and repetition seem undeniable. As Marx (2012: 49) rightly posits, AKB48 looks and sounds a great deal like Onyanko Club because they have the same producer, Akimoto Yasushi, who is a powerful player in the culture industry. Like Japanese idols more generally, the members of AKB48 are characterized by ordinary looks, less-than-stellar skills in singing and dancing, and a style that mixes innocence and sexuality. It is not the case, however, that Akimoto simply created stars by producing idols and pushing them into the ears and eyes and down the throats of the masses. To assume this would be to overestimate Akimoto and underestimate the audience. No, what Akimoto did was win over an audience by cultivating its relationships with idols, or turning the audience into a "fan audience" (Karlin 2012). In Akimoto's AKB business model generally and the General Election specifically, we see an ingenious system that stages encounters between idols and fans and capitalizes on affective relations between them. Even as idols compete with one another for the spotlight and for fans, fans have their *oshimen*, or "member I support," and compete to support them. This is institutionalized in the

General Election, which also shows how attraction to, affection for, and activity surrounding idols can be translated into CD sales.

Bringing in the critical approach of the Frankfurt School here proves useful. Consider how Horkheimer and Adorno understood the culture industry to be "artfully sanctioning the demand for trash," and, in so doing, "the system inaugurates total harmony" (Horkheimer and Adorno 2002: 106). Bracket out the totalizing rhetoric for a moment. Beyond the obvious point that the media and material culture associated with idols is not the most transcendent, Akimoto is part of a system that artfully sanctions the demand for trash, literally. He needed to sell CDs to please the establishment and needed to sell fans new ways to interact with idols and show their love, which he accomplished by making physical CDs into carriers for tickets to events and voting ballots. The CDs are disposable, and indeed fans buy in bulk, have no use for the discs after extracting the premiums, and subsequently dump them into the trashcan. One does not need more than one CD recording of the same song, but the need is, for lack of a better way to put it, "fabricated" (Horkheimer and Adorno 2002: 109). While a colossal waste of material resources, it serves the needs of a system in harmony.

In his influential critique of the Frankfurt School, Bernard Gendron asserts that, because music is not a disposable commodity, one would not buy the same music recording twice (Gendron 1986: 28), but this is precisely what is happening with AKB48. To be blunt, the CD is functional as the vehicle for the premium, every bit as much as the music recorded on it is textual; one does not have to like the music to buy more than one copy of the CD, because its function as a vehicle is more important than the music in deciding to make the purchase. Like the empty and disposable can of Comet detergent that Gendron imagines, fans toss the CDs out after they have extracted from them the premiums that make affective experiences with AKB48 possible. For those buying CDs for affective experiences facilitated by premiums, the content of the CD, or the music itself, is also somewhat disposable, as the next single replaces the last and allows for ongoing interactions and relations with idols.

As one can see from the AKB48 General Election, choice is built into the system. "Something is provided for everyone," Horkheimer and Adorno write, "so that no one can escape" (Horkheimer and Adorno 2002: 97). While perhaps guilty here again of a totalizing approach, the spirit of the critique can be appreciated with consideration of AKB48. With approximately 398 members (as of January 2019) in AKB48 and its sister groups in competition with one another, fans are free to choose a favorite.[5] Each member labors to stand out, win fans, and move up in the ranks. While in no way meaning to diminish the individuality of the members, there is clearly standardization in the AKB48 family, where young women come in, become idols, and then graduate out. It is as idols wearing similar uniforms and singing similar songs that AKB48 members compete, only to be replaced later as the group goes on in a continuous cycle of regeneration. While Akimoto is no longer as involved in the production process as he once was, the choices presented to fans are still produced members of the AKB48 family. Fans are free to choose, but they choose members of the AKB48 family. This is the same premise as the General Election: No matter whom fans choose from the wide range of candidates, they choose the AKB48 family, which wins.

So too does its producer, Akimoto, who bows to an election that he has set up and from which he profits.[6] In a similar way, Horkheimer and Adorno write, "The industry bows to the vote it has itself rigged" (Horkheimer and Adorno 2002: 106).

Again, one must be careful not to overestimate the industry and its "mass control" (Marx 2012: 37). Producers that claim this kind of influence are no doubt given to delusions of grandeur. Certainly not everyone is attracted to AKB48 or votes in the elections—most Japanese, in fact, do not. With 2,734,433 votes cast in the 2015 election out of a total Japanese population of 126,573,481, one must also keep in mind that the same people buying multiple copies of designated CDs cast many of the ballots. That said, it is hard not to see how the rhetoric of choice in the system, like the elections, can serve to obscure the power of the culture industry to produce and promote choices. Consider that in 2015, AKB48's biggest competition on the yearly Oricon Singles Chart was its own sister groups and a group identified as its "official rival" (*kōshiki raibaru*), which are all produced by Akimoto.[7]

While an excellent example in its own right, AKB48 shines a light on something beyond Japan and the present moment. Foundational work on the Hollywood star system suggests that it "never creates the star, but it proposes the candidate for 'election,' and helps to retain the favor of the 'electors'" (Franceso Alberoni, cited in Dyer 1979: 19). This approach accounts for the individual charisma and certain degree of chance involved in success, but does not overlook the power of those selecting people to put on stage and up for election. Furthermore, in his groundbreaking analysis in *The Image* (originally published in 1962), Daniel J. Boorstin writes that "each of us likes a movie star or television celebrity more when we think we have had a hand in making him a celebrity" (Boorstin 2012: 221). He highlights the example of a company staging a national election for a model to represent Rheingold beer in 1941. "By 1957, the 20,000,000 [votes] cast in the election of Miss Rheingold made it the largest election in the United States outside of that for President. The fact that customers were allowed to vote more than once simply added to the tantalizing verisimilitude" (Boorstin 2012: 221–22). As Boorstin rightly argues, active participation gets individuals more intimately and personally involved.

All of this sounds strikingly familiar, but more recent examples demonstrate even greater convergence. Similar to the AKB48 General Election, the highly successful television show *American Idol* (2002–16) allowed "America to choose." The model offers what Henry Jenkins calls a "fantasy of empowerment," and the "promise of participation helps build fan investments" (Jenkins 2006: 64).[8] In the case of *American Idol*, the audience was cultivated as fans in relation to idols and moved to action, with as many as twenty-four million votes placed in a single night in 2003 (Jenkins 2006: 89). It is significant that this analysis comes from Jenkins, one of the founders of fan studies in North America and someone often seen as opposed to the Frankfurt School generally and Adorno specifically (Hills 2002: 30–32). Recognizing that active audiences and productive consumers are valuable to the culture industry, Jenkins shows how fans are now being courted.

Building and maintaining a relationship with the consumer is precisely what one would expect of postindustrial capitalism (Lazzarato 1996: 140–141), and it is precisely what idols function to achieve in contemporary media and material culture. That is why so much of Jenkins's analysis is so hauntingly resonant in Japan, as the culture industry there has generally been extremely adept at deploying idols to cultivate fan audiences (Aoyagi 2005: 63; Lukács 2010a: 4, 23–24; Karlin 2012: 84–88). If, as Jenkins suggests, "affective economics sees active audiences as potentially valuable if they can be courted and won over" (Jenkins 2006: 64), then it is the idol that attracts and holds the audience so that they might be courted and won over. More immediately, it is the idol that does the courting and winning over of the fan, who is moved to tune in, show up, and make a purchase.

When considering the fact that idols and fans are all laboring to build and maintain relationships, which has only intensified with the introduction of social media, the complexity of all of this beyond what the Frankfurt School anticipated snaps into focus. No one forces the members of AKB48 to become idols, go up for election, and campaign, but their "choice" comes under pressure to succeed in the system of social and interactive media oriented toward winning fans, followers, and supporters. This can, and does, demand a great deal of them, which they offer "freely" as part of their affective labor (Terranova 2000: 51). Fans are similarly drawn into and entangled in relations that pressure them to support their idols by, for example, buying more and more CDs. This action can be further encouraged by seeing one's idol suffering defeat and being pushed down and out in the ranking, which is put on display in media representations of AKB48, for example, the "documentaries" that show how hard they work and high they aspire, and the live responses to election results, which show members weeping and begging for support.

None of this is to say that what idols and fans do in relation to one another is not valuable, productive, and meaningful in its own right and beyond economic measures, but considering the economics of affect is absolutely crucial to understanding why the camera not cutting away from the crying woman on stage is arguably more important than the content of the CD that one bought to vote for her or someone else. And who is on the stage and in the audience has much to do with who is not on the stage and in the spotlight, namely Akimoto Yasushi, who set up the system of participation in this moment in the first place. Certainly the affect economy "satisfies multiple players and institutions in mutual yet asymmetrical ways" (Takeyama 2010: 238), but ignoring producers because what we see on the stage and in the audience is so immediate, so real and raw, is a mistake. The intervention of the Frankfurt School and the culture industry as a concept points us toward a "critical political economy of media and communication" (Fuchs 2012). This intervention and its lessons are too often forgotten in the rush to celebrate consumers as productive, agentive, and active. While in no way arguing that consumers generally and fans specifically are anything otherwise, in the spirit of the Frankfurt School, one must ask how structures both enable and disable fan activity while valorizing it in particular ways.[9]

7 The Ordinary as Extraordinary

With the rise of affective economics, there has been a concomitant shift in audience desire for staged authenticity. Indeed, amateurism has come to be a valued quality in popular music today, whether in the proliferation of reality television music shows such as *The Voice* and *Pop Idol* or Japanese idol groups such as AKB48. The affective investment of fans in performers, through a process of identification, has created a new structure of patronage born from the greater demand for audience participation. Like systems of patronage that have subsequently arisen in social media, audiences have come to perceive themselves as coproducers in the process of media personalities, who are closer and more intimate with their audiences in terms of accessibility and ordinariness.

This leveling of differences between performers and audiences, and collapsing of the distance between them, has a long history in Japan's idol system. Significantly, the development of karaoke overlaps with the rise of idols from the 1970s, and both have contributed to the growth of amateur performers. In the 1980s, Onyanko Club was intentionally formed from amateurs, who were nevertheless consummate idols. Virtually anyone could sing and dance along with them; their concerts were a scene of mass karaoke, as fans joined them in an embodied and moving experience. By the 1990s,

J-pop increasingly was being produced with the intention of having it be consumed as a means of self-performance, expression, and communication among friends. In short, the songs were such that people could sing them together during karaoke (Sakakura 2014: 29). While songs requiring a wide range of pitch were not uncommon in J-pop of the time (e.g., Utada Hikaru), extremely difficult songs, which individuals and groups could not perform during karaoke, were in many cases avoided in favor of what could be reproduced by amateur singers. This was especially true in the case of idols such as Morning Musume, who were positioned between professional and amateur. Like a reality television show, Onyanko Club and Morning Musume inaugurated a new age of idols by creating the perception of greater audience participation. The culmination of the model of the idol as amateur performer is AKB48.[1]

Idols such as the members of AKB48 are about the process of "becoming." This begins from the radical idea that performers who are not fully developed and ready should be put on stage and allowed to fail, work it out, and grow under the watchful eye of the audience, whose support is won. There are three immediate consequences to this open process of becoming. First, it represents the emergence of a new kind of symbiotic relationship between performer and audience. Second, as unpolished amateur performers, idols are not expected to achieve perfection, but rather to become idols through an immanent process of self-refinement. The idol does not transform into something other, but rather is expected to refine her character through perseverance and hard work. Idols are presented as flawed, inexperienced, and struggling to succeed, which makes them relatable, approachable, and likeable. As that which is cute or lovable, desire for the idol is immanent. Third, idols such as the members of AKB48 begin as, or are presented as, adolescent females whose transition into sexuality is measured across their careers. With many graduating at around the age of nineteen, the female idol's career maps closely to her becoming a sexualized woman.[2]

Consider again the formation of AKB48, but this time with an emphasis on how the original members came together in Akihabara in 2005. The recruitment of AKB48's first members commenced early that year with the establishment of a website, to which links were posted at various cafés in Akihabara, as well as the more standard procedure of taking out ads for auditions in entertainment magazines. As a testament to the aspirational desire to become an idol among young Japanese women (more on this in Chapter 10), 7,924 applied to audition. The number of applicants was whittled down by staff, who prioritized the applicants based on their photographs, age, and talents. The photographs were one of the most important criteria, but with numerous judges reviewing the applications, the goal was to select candidates of varying attractiveness that appealed to assorted tastes (i.e., to provide "something for everyone"). As for age, only those under twenty or twenty-one were considered, but some applicants were as young as ten or eleven years old. Since the age of majority in Japan is twenty, parental consent was required for most applicants. The audition of forty-five finalists was held on October 30, 2005.

Note that the emphasis was not necessarily on the best singers and dancers, and that recruiting idols in cafés in Akihabara suggests something other than a hunt for polished professionals with experience in the music and entertainment industries. Recruiting ordinary young women, as well as those with experience interacting with the men who were to be the core fan base, was by design part of the audition process. By foregoing more established artist management agencies (*jimusho*) and instead recruiting aspiring idols into his own agency (AKS), Akimoto deliberately sought out for AKB48 amateurs with no formal affiliations or experience. At the first audition, most of the applicants had never sung for such a large audience before. For many, their only prior singing experience was karaoke with family and friends. Fittingly enough, the audition process required a sort of karaoke performance, or singing along with prerecorded back tracks of popular songs.

In selecting women without professional experience, and younger women, the aim was to ensure what Akimoto Yasushi describes as a "roughness" (*dekoboko*) of character and appearance (Akimoto and Tahara 2013: 24). The "rough" character of the idol, and her unpolished performance, is essential to a perceived authenticity. One of the first members recruited to AKB48, Takahashi Minami, explains that "it's better to not be too good . . . since no one will follow you if you are perfect" (quoted in Akimoto and Tahara 2013: 180). Here Takahashi underscores how the imperfect idol is open to relations and in need of support in her process of becoming, which is an appeal distinct from facing a "complete" or "perfect" being. For his part, Akimoto differentiates the idol from the superstar or pop diva, whose image is honed to such perfection that only a highly fabricated performance remains. With pop divas, all aspects of the performance, ranging from hair and makeup to singing and dancing, aim for flawless perfection. In contrast, Akimoto likens the image of the idol to that of "the high-school girl who, having just finished her after-school club activities, runs on stage barely in the nick of time with her hair disheveled, covered in sweat, and still wearing her uniform" (Akimoto and Tahara 2013: 26). Note the ordinariness of the imagined individual, how incredibly hard she works, and the fact that blemishes show through as she rushes from one place to another, unprepared and dripping with sweat. By placing her within the context of everyday life in Japan, the ordinariness of the idol is a version of the archetypal "girl next door." It is precisely this ordinariness that is the hallmark of AKB48—just as it has been the hallmark of idols more generally since they first appeared in the 1970s.

In this way, the members of AKB48 are average but more "real," whereas professional artists are spectacular but "inhuman" (Atwood 2007: 449). This is pronounced in the reception of some North American artists in Japan, who seem somehow otherworldly. The authenticity and everydayness of idols such as the members of AKB48 is often set against the artificiality of professional artists, but this is not uniquely "Japanese." The desire for authenticity that contributes to the attraction of AKB48 is part of the turn toward ordinariness reflected in reality television and talent shows, to say nothing of influencers on social media.[3] Much like how "amateur" pornography claims to be better in its putative authenticity (Frith 2015: 389), idols are the "amateurs" of Japanese music and entertainment.

On the generation of desire, the bodies of idols such as the members of AKB48 are both sexualized and prohibited. From Yamaguchi Momoe's "Unripe Fruit" (*Aoi kajitsu*, 1973) and Onyanko Club's "Don't Make Me Take Off My Sailor Suit" (*Sērāfuku wo nugasanai de*, 1985) to AKB48's "My Uniform is Getting in the Way" (*Seifuku ga jama wo suru*, 2007), the transition into sexuality is a distinct dimension of the image of the female idol. With most of the lyrics of AKB48's songs written by Akimoto, fantasy is projected onto the idols through the songs they sing as well as the chastity that they are expected to uphold. The group's unofficial "no dating policy" (*renai kinshi jōrei*) exists as an informal mechanism for constraining the sexuality of its female performers.[4] The contradiction between sexualization and prohibition is further exacerbated by the appearance of AKB48 members in swimwear and lingerie in their music videos, photo albums, and "image videos," as well as glossy spreads in various weekly magazines.[5] Unlike so-called gravure idols, whose career centers on posing for pin-up photos and showing off impressive figures, the members of AKB48 maintain their pure image while simultaneously revealing their bodies (never quite completely). These images of AKB48 circulate as tokens of a highly erotic yet unadorned reality, which signify authenticity through ordinariness. The appeal of softcore images of idols arises from the authenticity of their unrefined amateurism.

So it is that the idol industry, like the culture industry, is simultaneously "pornographic and prudish," even as the "mass production of sexuality automatically brings about its repression" (Horkheimer and Adorno 2002: 111–12).[6] In this way, the idol is both innocent and sexualized, child and adult, sold as sexual fantasy but punished for having sex in reality. In the regular scandals for which female idols seem almost destined (Prusa 2012: 57, 60), one can see how media and material culture take on "the quality of organized cruelty" (Horkheimer and Adorno 2002: 110).

This was on full display in 2013, when a video of AKB48 member Minegishi Minami's apology to her fans was posted on the group's official webpage (Figure 3). After a tabloid

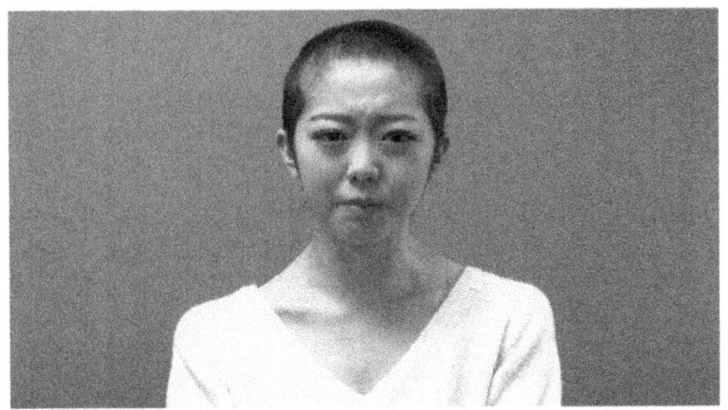

Figure 3 *AKB48 member Minegishi Minami apologizes for violating the group's unofficial "no dating policy."*

Source: AKB48, "AKB48 Minegishi Minami kara no messēji," January 31, 2013, https://web.archive.org/web/20130131105430/https://www.youtube.com/watch?v=UlzrlgacADU.

newspaper published photographs of her leaving the apartment of a male idol, with whom she had spent the night, Minegishi decided to shave her head in an act of contrition. As one of the original and longest-serving members of AKB48, Minegishi's apology was part of a spectacle of ritualized redemption. She was not expelled from the group, but rather sent back to the lowest level and allowed to work to redeem herself in the eyes of fans (Sakakura 2014: 3–8). If one takes votes in the General Election to be any indicator, Minegishi went down in ranking, but was still near the top; so her story, her becoming, continued.[7] In this way, idols flame out, fall and rise again, persevere. It is as predictable as it is "cathartic" (Horkheimer and Adorno 2002: 122–24), because it all appears to be so real. Indeed, struggles and tears have a place in the idol system generally and AKB48 specifically.

8 Tears of the Idol

One of the most conspicuous things that idols such as the members of AKB48 do is cry. An important expression demanded of female idols in Japan, shedding tears is part of the labor that these idols perform for fans. Performances at the AKB48 Theater are opportunities for members to talk and express emotions, both to their fans and to one another. Between the singing and dancing are structured occasions for crying. An event marking the graduation of a member, for example, is certain to conclude with singing through tears. Such public displays of emoting are shared on and off stage, as idols and fans are moved and cry together.

An even more striking emotional event is the AKB48 General Election. When results are announced at a live ceremony, each member is expected to give a short speech. Reflecting on those that voted for her and her rank vis-à-vis other members as she addresses fans, the idol sobs (Figures 4, 5, and 6). As tears stream down her cheeks, the idol is described as human, authentic, and even cute (i.e., lovable).[1] In these moments of crying, she appeals to her fans and elicits a powerful response. They may cry with her at the event and in places and times beyond it. Watching a video of the General Election with the authors in 2011, a male fan of AKB48 commented, "No matter how many times I watch this, it makes me cry." More specifically, he went on, seeing his idol cry in this moment of her career made him cry. He felt for and with her; he was moved. Interestingly, this came with a strong desire to support and care for his idol, who in her vulnerability needed him.

Figures 4, 5, and 6 *Takahashi Minami, Watanabe Mayuko, and Ōshima Yūko (from top to bottom) address their fans at the AKB48 General Election held at Ajinomoto Stadium in Tokyo on June 7, 2014.*

Source: Documentary of AKB48 The Time Has Come: Shōjo-tachi wa, ima, sono senaka ni nani wo omou?, Blu-Ray, directed by Takahashi Eiki (Tokyo: Tōhō, 2014).

Tears are a common theme in postwar Japanese popular music, including both *enka* and J-pop. Lyrics about crying are so common in *enka*—a modern popular music genre that evokes "traditional" Japan—that it has become a cliché. As Christine R. Yano notes, these lyrics about crying are often in songs that seek to get listeners crying, since the merits of an *enka* song generally are measured by its ability to elicit tears (Yano 2002: 4, 98). In 1950, Minami Hiroshi conducted a survey of Japanese popular songs (*ryūkōka*) and found that "crying" (*naku*) was an overwhelmingly common verb in lyrics (Minami 2012: 164–65). In a similar study conducted in 1970, the results again confirmed the importance of crying (Minami 1979: 130–33). And an even more recent study found that "crying" and "tears" (*namida*) were two of the most common lyrics in J-pop songs across the entire period from 1968 to 2011 (Onozawa 2013: 70). Of the first thirty-six official singles of AKB48, the lyrics of fourteen mention "crying" or "tears."

Even as crying and tears are prohibited in so many other parts of life, especially in front of others (Ekman and Friesen 2003: 23–24), they are encouraged for AKB48 idols, who in turn encourage them among fans. According to Tada Michitarō, tears represent surrender to the social order (Tada 1990: 220–21). He argues that we identify not with the suffering of others, but rather with the difficulty of constraining our emotions. The ease with which tears are induced through the spectacle of suffering is explained by Tada's assertion that crying is a form of release. When tears are shed this way, the individual does not necessarily identify with the suffering of others, but rather the liminal context wherein the expression of emotion is sanctioned. The shedding of tears is an emotional release, which idols facilitate.

A cynical reading of Tada and tears as surrender to the social order might well bring to mind catharsis and Horkheimer and Adorno (2002: 122–23), who highlight "tragedy ... as routine" in situations where "everyone knows that they are helpless within the system, and ideology must take account of this." Simply put, facing the tragedies seen in mass entertainment and having a good cry is part of what cements us into place and keeps us in line. Early studies of soap operas and melodrama similarly saw tear-jerking narratives as a way for women to come to terms with their place in the social order and world, but things were rarely so straightforward. Indeed, despite their bald disdain for the content and its target demographic, one of the few seemingly sympathetic examples that Horkheimer and Adorno (2002: 111, 123) give in their critique of mass culture is women finding moments of release.[2] The rich literature on soap operas and melodrama came to explore complex and contradictory readings of tears as not only surrender but also resistance, self-care, and more (Ang 1990: 165; Fiske 1994: 244; Blumenthal 1997: 56).

In the case of AKB48, we were personally struck by the way that idols moved fans and allowed them to cry openly in public. This is all the more noteworthy in the case of adult men like the one described above, who cried while watching his idol cry. We do not mean to diminish the significance of those tears, but continue to wonder with Horkheimer, Adorno, and Tada how the movements of idols and fans are nested and channeled. Shedding tears was something increasingly asked of AKB48 as they rose to prominence in the Japanese media system in the 2010s, which raises questions about the order in which they were embedded and their status as public figures.

9 The Labor of Love

From the lost decade of the 1990s onward, Japan has seen a rapid and sustained increase in temporary and irregular employment, but it is worth noting that concern about this is most often biased toward young men. As Laura Fantone (2005: 7) argues, recent debates on precarious labor arose only when the "male worker began feeling the negative effects of the new post-industrial, flexible job market." For their part, idols are quintessential precarious workers, whose careers are short lived and without any assurances of regularity. They are also emblematic of new forms of immaterial and affective labor in postindustrial Japan. They are agents of the immaterial paradigm of labor that "produces the informational and cultural content of the commodity form," and are affective laborers, who rely on interaction and symbolic exchange for the "creation and manipulation of affects" (Hardt 1999: 95).

With the understanding that this condition of labor is not just exploitation and not limited to women (Takeyama 2010: 237–40), we nonetheless argue that the production and reproduction of laboring bodies in the affect economy should not be waved away as simply about choice, opportunity, and pleasure.[1] Having observed the members of AKB48 in their relations with producers, media, and fans, not to mention one another, we could not agree more with Gabriella Lukács (2015: 496–97) that performing as cute or lovable is a form of labor. Indeed, at times of peak fan interaction such as the General Election, the members of AKB48 appear absolutely exhausted by the demands of always being "on." With cameras everywhere, there is little opportunity to relax. Consider then the added pressure to devote "free" time and "extra" energy to engage with fans on social media. If users of social media that do not intend for it to be work complain of "fatigue," "exhaustion," and "burnout" (Ravindran et al. 2014), then all the more so for idols as professionals of cuteness. Is it really any mystery why the majority of them can only keep it up for a few years?[2]

Even the carefully crafted "documentaries," which are actually idol promotional material, show Maeda Atsuko and Ōshima Yūko collapsing behind the scenes (Takahashi 2012; Takahashi 2013).[3] Responding to this, labor activist Amamiya Karin comments, "How many people know the extent that these women are 'worldly wise?'"[4] The *kanji* corresponding to "worldly wise" are more literally translated as "pain, anguish, suffering" (*ku*), "labor" (*rō*), and "person or people" (*nin*), which strips away some of their romance. This would seem to be an indictment of the whole operation, but in fact serves as the opposite; Amamiya's comment was included as catch copy on posters for the documentaries in front of theaters around Tokyo. There is a beauty in the suffering—in all the sweat and tears—to achieve one's dreams. Even as AKB48 songs are often about labor and sometimes appear quite critical (Sakakura 2014: 8–11), there is still the message, as Horkheimer and Adorno (2002: 122) might put it, that, "Such is the world—so hard, yet therefore so wonderful, so healthy." The idols of AKB48 labor and suffer like us, for us—they are us, only healthier and more beautiful in the spotlight.

As Lukács highlights, affective labor is seen as more rewarding and fulfilling than other forms of labor in the service economy, and such "dreamwork" feeds into the "dream factory"

(Lukács 2013: 49, 52–54, 58–60; also Takeyama 2010; Ho 2012b).
Is it any surprise, then, that when Miura Atsushi surveyed
young people about jobs that they would like to try, most
chose occupations that have to do with performance such
as acting, modeling, and singing (Miura 2008: 107)?[5] Even the
lowest-ranked members of AKB48 act as success stories that
keep people dreaming and performing their own cuteness
and affective labor.

Earlier, we described what idols do in relation to fans and
one another as "the labor of love." This is intended to express
how idols and fans labor doing what they love and labor for
love. Rather than passive dupes, idols and fans actively and
knowingly labor in the affect economy, or labor for love.
Corporations act as apparatuses to capture some of the value
generated by idols and fans in relation to one another; idols,
fans, and their relations are supported by corporations, which
they in turn support. This model allows us to consider how the
labor of love takes place within a system that Tiziana Terranova
argues "nurtures, exploits, and exhausts" (Terranova 2000: 51).
The labor of love sustains and supports life as it simultaneously
drains and depletes it.

What might the labor of love look like? Perhaps like Ōshima
Yūko campaigning for votes as an expression of love in the
General Election. Or rival Maeda Atsuko crying on stage after
defeating her in the General Election and telling fans that they
can hate her, but not AKB48, which is a platform for the labor
of love.[6] Or perhaps how all of these AKB48 idols laboring for
love inspire their fans to love, live, and labor on, which Hamano
Satoshi proposes to be a function mirroring religion (Hamano
2012: 166–67, 174–75). Fans buying multiple CDs to vote for
an idol, then gifting the extra ones, because they do not want

to be bad fans who waste the material, and also imagine that sharing it might spread the love and bring others into the fold of AKB48. Fans chanting, jumping, shouting, and gesticulating at live events, those ritual spectacles of intimacy, where idols on stage perhaps notice them and smile. Idols shaking the hands of hundreds, even thousands of fans who have lined up to express their love. Fans singing idol songs at karaoke and dancing along at concerts.

We might also ask if there are ways to engage in the labor of love that are less directly linked to the demands of the system. For example, after detailing how AKB48 members are systematically subjected to stress and failure, which is then taken to be their fault, Sakakura Shōhei draws attention to the phenomenon of idols refusing to be exhausted. In stark contrast to the center and select group, there are many members of AKB48 categorized as "non-elite" (*non'eriito*), or those of low or virtually no rank. While Akimoto Yasushi once demanded that such idols participate in the General Election and simply try harder, they are now allowed to drop out while remaining in the AKB48 family (Sakakura 2014: 244–45, 256–57, 262–63). These non-elite members remain idols for their fans, however small in number, even as this does not do much for AKB48's bottom line. Setting limits, withdrawing from competition, and preserving themselves, these idols are finding "ways to live as non-elites" (Sakakura 2014: 249–50)—something they share with supporters, whose lives they in turn support. If affective labor produces "collective subjectivities" and "sociality," as Michael Hardt (1999: 89) suggests, then we see here how "affective labor is simultaneously more exploitative and more conducive to experimentation with new forms of political engagement," as Lukács (2013: 48) would argue. These nascent alternatives, however encouraging, have yet to fundamentally change the AKB48 system and should not blind us to the ways that the labor of love is channeled and valorized. Two such ways are idol-fan activities and political activism, which are taken up in the following chapters.

10 Female Fans as Aspirational Consumers

As AKB48 attempted to expand beyond its largely male fan base and appeal to female consumers in the 2010s, advertising agencies saw potential. Producer Akimoto Yasushi actively hyped up the group, boasting that the biggest result of advertising with AKB48 is that they "move product" (Akimoto 2012: 29). Some metrics seem to bear this out. In 2011, confection manufacturer Ezaki Glico called on AKB48 for an advertising campaign for one of its ice cream products, which had long been popular with female consumers; its sales increased by 150 percent (Kon 2012). This increase, however, appears more due to the spectacle of the AKB48 advertising campaign than to a specific appeal to women (Figure 7).[1]

Although Akimoto touted AKB48 as effective at promoting nearly any product or service, appealing directly to girls and women with the idols as aspirational models had mixed results. The members of AKB48 first appeared on the cover of popular women's magazine *anan* in 2010, when it was hoped that they would appeal to readers as models of feminine beauty. For her part, Maeda Atsuko expressed concern about being depicted as an ideal of female attractiveness.[2] When Maeda ("Acchan" to fans) appeared the next year on the cover of the teen girls' magazine *Love Berry* in 2011, the captions shouted, "Why is she so cute!?" and "I want to be like Acchan!" Besides

Figure 7 *Maeda Atsuko appears in this murder mystery-themed series of TV commercials for Ezaki Glico in 2012.*

Source: Ezaki Glico, "AKB48 satsujin jiken," television advertisement, June 25, 2012.

Maeda, Matsui Jurina (SKE48), Maeda Ami (AKB48), and Itano Tomomi (AKB48) also featured prominently in the magazine. In March 2012, *Love Berry* ceased publication due to poor sales. Although changes in the magazine market were no doubt a contributing factor, the deployment of AKB48 family members did not magically "move product" as Akimoto promised. More bluntly stated, the power of early AKB48 members to appeal to women was overstated. Calling them "role models" was often more prescriptive than descriptive at the time.

In contrast, members of "rival" groups, particularly Nogizaka46 (from an upscale neighborhood in Tokyo), began finding success appearing on the covers of women's magazines. Members of Nogizaka46 such as Hashimoto Nanami, Matsumura Sayuri, Nishino Nanase, and Shiraishi Mai all have contracts as models with women's fashion magazines. Their sleek appearance and style have attracted women, who look to these idols as models of fashion and cuteness. The success of Nogizaka46, including sales of their CDs, has come mostly from the growing number of female fans; at handshake events for Nogizaka46, roughly 20 percent to 30 percent of the attendees are female fans.[3] These female fans of Nogizaka46 not only engage in the same activities of supporting idols as male fans, including buying multiple copies of CDs and attending events, but also consume the magazines and products they advertise; the power of Shiraishi Mai ("Maiyan" to fans) to generate sales of the clothes she wears is so great that it has its own term ("Maiyan-ure," or Maiyan sales). This is great news for advertising agencies such as Dentsu, which count on idols to reach female consumers (Karlin 2012).

In a broader sense, idols are rapidly becoming aspirational models for young women in Japan—an aspect of idol culture since the 1970s, but in ways that seem more intensive than before. During the boom that followed the mainstream breakout of AKB48 in the early 2010s, when so many groups competed for national supremacy that some dubbed it "the idol warring states period" (*aidoru sengoku jidai*), the number of young women that wanted to become idols skyrocketed. In addition to the surge in new idol groups signed to agencies— according to one estimate, nearly 1,000 female idol groups (Craig and Zhang 2017: 80)—an excess of wannabes founded or joined underground/indies idol groups, the number of which ballooned from around 50 in Tokyo in 2008 to over 350 in 2015.[4] A few might make it big, most will transition into other occupations after graduating from high school or college, and some will continue in their idol activities while working part-time jobs. As aspirational models, the female idol produces and codifies notions of femininity through the repetition of gender performance and promotes the fantasy of employment in the entertainment industry.

Embarking on a career as an idol has become something casual, which is even supported by institutions of higher education. In 2011, universities across Japan began to register new after-school clubs, whose activities included watching idol music videos, learning the dances, and performing them for others. These clubs wanted to come together and perform for larger audiences, and, in 2012, UNIDOL was born.[5] Short for "university idol," UNIDOL is an event that brings together student groups that perform "cover dances of idol groups" (*aidoru gurūpu no kopī dansu*) and puts them in competition with one another for the honor of being named number one in Japan.[6] In 2015, Okada Kōhei, then a student at Meiji University and chairman of the UNIDOL Executive Committee, explained that "in the 1990s, during the band boom, a lot of cover bands appeared in Japan. In the same way, cover idols have increased during the idol boom. Some of them don't stop at the hobby and go on to be active as underground idols."[7]

Despite these connections to the industry, Okada stresses that members of the cover dance groups that perform at UNIDOL are university students and "idol fans" (*aidoru fan*). That is, they aspire to be idols, but perform without necessarily devoting themselves to this professionally. The official website lays out the narrative as follows: "For one night only, ordinary women enrolled in universities stand on stage as 'idols.'"[8] Note, first, the insistence that they are "ordinary women enrolled in universities" (*futsū no joshi daisei*), and second, the way that "idol" is placed in scare quotes. Another intended meaning of UNIDOL is apparently "un-idol," which is a neologism explained in Japanese as *"aidoru dewanai,"* or "not an idol." The explanation continues, "They are not idols, but they are cute."[9]

Even as Okada both acknowledges and denies links to the professional idol industry, the narrative laid out on the UNIDOL official website masks the labor of love performed over time with a Cinderella-like dream of one-night transformation. As amateurs performing their labor of love, these young women nonetheless function as idols in the evolving industry. Idol fans engage in cover dance performances because it is "fun" (*tanoshii*), and they do it as part of after-school club activities, but at the same time these activities are serious business. The UNIDOL finals, for example, have evolved into a major media event covered by an estimated 150 outlets, including television stations TV Tokyo and BS Fuji; print media such as *Mainichi Shimbun*, *Sankei Shimbun*, and *Weekly Playboy*; and websites Jiji.com, Mantan TV, MSN Video, Yahoo! News, Nico Nico News, and Excite News, among many others.[10] Tickets are sold, there are corporate sponsors, and professional idol groups appear as guests and presenters. In both 2017 and 2018, for example, members of AKB48 sister groups stood on stage with young women that performed their dances at the UNIDOL finals.

Interest in university-aged women as potential idols is certainly not without precedent in Japan (Okada 2008: 93), but rather than being scouted and produced by agencies for magazines or television, ordinary young women are now producing and performing themselves as idols. This is a phenomenon of fandom, not agencies and advertisers, and it is spreading across the nation. As of December 2018, UNIDOL was being held twice a year, in addition to special events for first-year students and those about to graduate; it had also spun off events such as Highdol, which features high-school students; UNIBOY, for male students in university; and UNI♡KP, devoted to those performing cover dances of K-pop idols. With preliminaries held around the country, well over 20,000 performers were involved each year.[11] All this feeds into the idol system, as these idol-fan performers cover the dances and advertise the songs, reinforce interest in idols, and themselves function as idols in both amateur and professional contexts.[12] That the line between AKB48 and them is blurring is precisely the point, even as more and more young women try out for a spot in the ever growing AKB48 family. This is one way that the labor of love is being channeled and valorized in contemporary Japan, but it is not the only one.

11 Placebo Idols

Beyond consumption and cuteness, idols can also function to model caring behavior. In their role as purported "national idols" (*kokumin-teki aidoru*), the members of AKB48 are expected to affirm their status in the national community through the performance of public service, especially public expressions of grief at times of national crisis (Karlin 2016: 33). This was the case in the fallout of the triple disaster—earthquake, tsunami, and meltdown of a nuclear power plant—that struck the Tōhoku region of northern Japan on March 11, 2011, when AKB48 played a prominent role in promoting charity and relief.

In the weeks after what came to be known as "3.11," a mood of self-restraint engulfed the Japanese nation, and it became increasingly difficult for idols to appear in the public sphere unless their promotional activities were in some way tied to charity events or relief efforts.[1] The AKB48 Theater was immediately closed and, within three days of the triple disaster, the production company of AKB48 announced the cancellation of the group's planned concerts to be held at the Yokohama Arena later that month. In addition, the release of the group's third album—scheduled for April 6— was postponed, and related promotional handshake and photo events were also canceled.[2] With the Yokohama Arena already reserved for their planned events, the only way to salvage losses was to do something else there in the name of charity. The group's official blog explained the decision to hold a charity event as "a way of responding to the appeals of the group's members and demands of fans."[3] To counter criticisms that such an event would be wasteful of electricity amid national efforts to conserve power after the meltdown at the nuclear plant in Tōhoku, the event would not use stage elevators and would utilize half the number of lights at 50 percent brightness. In the end, the concert was converted into a charity fundraising event for soliciting donations and selling leftover commemorative goods.

Instead of appearing at the opening night of the charity event, AKB48 members made their first public appearance at a hastily arranged charity concert in the southernmost prefecture of Okinawa, where concerns about power conservation were unlikely to raise eyebrows. In addition to collecting donations, twelve top members performed three songs, including one that was to be released as the group's "charity song." Proceedings from the sale of the song were donated entirely to charity (in theory, anyway, as we will discuss later). The song, "For Someone" (*Dareka no tame ni*, 2011), was repurposed from the group's catalogue and rereleased to serve as the name for the group's charitable project. In addition to sixty-six visits to local communities and schools affected by the triple disaster, the For Someone Project raised more than ¥1.3 billion (about US$13 million) for disaster relief (as of June 2018).

Despite lingering concerns about power shortages and rolling blackouts, AKB48 performed three days of concerts on July 22, 23, and 24, 2011, at the Seibu Dome in Saitama Prefecture. During the second day of the concert, Maeda Atsuko, who was at the time the center of the group, collapsed backstage. Although it was announced during the concert that Maeda was suffering from heat exhaustion, she made a triumphant return at the end of the concert to perform the group's latest single. Later it was revealed that in addition to Maeda, several other members had collapsed from heat exhaustion. Reports in the media and by fans of the group on social media cast Maeda's return to the stage as a demonstration of "professional spirit" (*puro konjō*). The teamwork of the members coming together to overcome the challenges of performing a grueling schedule in the intense summer heat highlighted the importance of sacrifice. In an interview on August 21, producer Akimoto explained that, for fans, "seeing the girls persevere makes them want to work harder."[4] Attributing the success of the group to their "dedication," Akimoto praised Maeda and deftly shifted the emphasis from professionalism to spirit. As he saw it, "While professionals are often expected to pace themselves, giving it your all is what AKB is all about."

The difficulties of the Seibu Dome concert figured prominently in the group's promotional film *Documentary of AKB48 Show Must Go On*, which opened in theaters on January 27, 2012. The narrative stresses the importance of perseverance amid the national crisis. Utilizing 3.11, *Show Must Go On* intercuts scenes of the group's numerous visits to the disaster area and the struggles of members as they perform in concerts and compete in the annual election. The framing device that opens and concludes the documentary is the personal story of Iwata Karen, who qualified to audition to become a "research student" (*kenkyūsei*) less than one month before 3.11. Iwata is from the city of Sendai in Miyagi Prefecture, and was the only member of AKB48 directly affected by the disaster. Her story about persisting to become a new member of the group, though filled with thoughts of family and home, is but one of the personal stories interwoven into a narrative of suffering and sacrifice. Although the audition was to be held on March 13, it was postponed due to the earthquake until April. The documentary concludes with Iwata resolving to continue with the audition, feeling that it is the best way to bring happiness to the people in her hometown. In one scene, during the group's seventh visit to the disaster area, Iwata is joined by several of the group's more senior members on a visit to see "the miracle pine" (*kiseki no ippon-matsu*) in Rikuzentakata City, Iwate Prefecture. The tree, which is described as the "the tree of hope" by the city's mayor, was "the one lone pine tree out of 70,000 that survived the tsunami."[5] The image seeks to connect the tree as a symbol of perseverance to the personal narratives of AKB48 members and their personal struggles (Figure 8).

Rather than reflecting on the hardships of the disaster on its victims, the seven visits to the Tōhoku region depicted in

Figure 8 *Iwata Karen, an AKB48 "research student," looks upon "the miracle pine" in Rikuzentakata City, Iwate Prefecture.*

Source: Documentary of AKB48 Show Must Go On: Shōjo-tachi wa kizutsukinagara, yume wo miru, Blu-ray, directed by Takahashi Eiki (Tokyo: Tōhō, 2012).

Show Must Go On are entirely shot from the perspective of the idols. Without transition, the documentary intersperses footage of the visits to the disaster area with scenes of the idols' own tribulations. Takajō Aki, for example, is shown twisting her ankle just prior to the General Election in June. The idols commiserate about how "difficult" (*kurushii*) it is to hear the results of the election. In another scene, the members are scolded by producer Akimoto following the first day of the Seibu Dome concert for being disorganized and unprepared. During rehearsals, Maeda becomes anxious to the extent of hyperventilating, at which point she is shown being carried away on a stretcher. Throughout, the hardships of the idols appear continuous with the suffering of the victims of the triple disaster. By association, *Show Must Go On* connotes that the idols found the strength to persevere in their own personal struggles by witnessing the hardships of the victims during their visits to the Tōhoku region. Similarly, the idols rationalize their highly publicized visits as having "brought smiles to the faces" of the victims.

In most amateur footage of the tsunami, which was rebroadcast by many news networks and also often circulated as videos on the internet, one almost never sees the reactions of those in the midst of the crisis. The camera is focused from a distance on the encroaching waves as they engulf coastal towns. The voices of survivors huddled on the roofs of buildings or promontories outside the reach of the waves are heard, but one rarely sees the suffering on their faces behind the lens of the camera. Similar to these amateur videos, the AKB48 "documentary" never permits the audience to see and feel the suffering of those directly impacted by the disaster. Instead, it substitutes the idols for the victims. Surveying the destruction out the window of a tour bus, the experience of the suffering and hardship of the disaster is reflected in the eyes of the idol, even as they suffer as performers. It is not the destruction itself that is the object of the camera's gaze, but rather the way in which that destruction is embodied and materialized in the idol and her gaze. The intense materiality of emotion is registered in the sullen and tearful expressions of the idol. As a spectacle of suffering, the idol responding to disaster is meant to resonate with Japanese audiences.

In the context of charity events, the tears of idols are conflated with an emotional appeal to help and support the community. The idol cries for others, as discussed earlier, but here her act goes beyond moving the fan to offer his care and support for the performer or performers. In their response to 3.11, the members of AKB48, like other "national idols" at the time, functioned as professional mourners—a phenomenon seen throughout history and among different cultures. In Ancient Greece, Rome, and the Middle East, professional mourners were paid to amplify feelings of loss and to dignify the tears of the bereaved (Lutz 1999: 200). During the middle ages, those who came to funerals and feigned grief in hopes of receiving food and drink were disparaged as "placebo singers."[6] Seen as insincere and opportunistic, these professional mourners were grouped together with other degraded professions such as usury. As professional mourners, there is a similar danger for the members of AKB48 to be taken as "placebo idols." The subsequent demand for authenticity is also a demand for them to labor for love, which is valorized in specific ways.

In the wake of 3.11, many of Japan's television broadcast networks, talent agencies, and other media companies created

AKB48

accounts in order to collect donations. Instead of soliciting direct donations to established charitable foundations such as the Red Cross, many idols solicited donations to the bank accounts of their agencies.[7] By collecting donations on behalf of its fans, AKB48 was able to take tax deductions for the amount they collected, but after first paying as much as 50 percent of it as a gift tax (*zōyozei*) to the national government.[8] Tax deductions were an incentive to collect donations, but the most significant benefit was the publicity and good will that it garnered them in the media. By announcing massive donations to charity to support the victims of 3.11, charity served as an important tool of public relations and promotion. In this way, the accumulated donations, which were presented as the labor of love of AKB48, provided an opportunity for their production agency to make public announcements to the press about their charitable activities. This kept the name of AKB48 in the spotlight while confirming their public service to the nation.

A common critique of celebrity advocacy is that it often amounts to little more than tragedy voyeurism. The proliferation of celebrity advocacy in the media perhaps reflects a weakening of the public sphere. As the public's attention becomes centered on celebrities as objects of affect and identification, the audience is increasingly interpellated as fans and consumers rather than citizens. While many critics are cynical about motives, celebrity involvement is often important for raising awareness of an overlooked issue or problem.[9] However, in a study that focused on public responses to celebrity advocacy in the United Kingdom, Dan Brockington and Spensor Henson (2015) found that celebrity alone did not guarantee media attention and that celebrity was a poor vehicle for promoting political advocacy. Not only might audiences be skeptical of celebrity advocacy and question the motivations for their involvement, but audiences, particularly fans, might also be interested more in the activities of celebrities than the charitable causes they are advocating.[10] Brockington and Henson state that the belief in celebrity advocacy as a means of attracting mass public support relates to how celebrities have come to signify the public: "Celebrity advocacy is thus bound up in, if not actively promoting, a post-democratic form of politics, with minimal actual involvement of citizens" (Brockington and Henson 2015: 445). The structural problems at the root of most charitable causes cannot be solved by donations and require political action. The focus on celebrities soliciting donations promotes a simplified understanding that suggests that complex issues can be resolved merely by giving money to idols.

In the case of 3.11, the role of Japanese idols was not necessarily to raise awareness of the triple disaster, which dominated the news cycle for months. Their knowledge of the catastrophe did not authorize them to better speak on behalf of the victims. These idols could only mobilize their fan networks to make charitable donations. Much as they function in advertising to sell goods and services, they moved their fans to engage in action that would confirm their identity as a fan or supporter. This blurring of the boundaries between affect and activism, whether for consumption or charity, demonstrates the limitations of fan activism to issues of social and political engagement (Burwell and Boler 2008). For those that donated money, charity was often a secondary consideration to the affective relationship to the idol that solicited their donations.

Like a handshake event or other opportunity promising greater intimacy, the fan was engaged in an affective exchange.

Celebrities facilitate the process of trust in giving, but are arguably problematic when soliciting donations as intermediaries. Just as the distinction between labor and leisure, paid and unpaid work, and production and consumption has disappeared, charity (*jizen*) and self-promotion (*gizen*) are also thoroughly entangled today. While the charitable donations and events of AKB48 undoubtedly helped raise money to promote recovery in the Tōhoku region, they also promoted the image of AKB48. With celebrities and idols appearing to endorse and promote goods and services for multiple corporate sponsors, charity is but another form of publicity. Owing to the flows of information in our networked society, the promotion of the status of idols through charitable activities also enhanced the image of the corporate sponsors through their mutual association. This is yet another way that the affective labor of idols, their labor of love, is channeled and valorized today. As hinted at in the discussion of charity, however, idols can repulse critics as powerfully as they attract fans. This tension becomes all the more obvious when idols such as AKB48 are taken or made to represent "Japan."

12 AKB48 in the Global Imagination

The topic of affective alliances encounters some interesting eddies around AKB48 in Japan and beyond. On the one hand, they certainly do seem to reinforce investments in the Japanese media-commodity system (Lukács 2010a: 54), perhaps even more so than idols as intertextual image-commodities, because of the insistence on being there, seeing and being seen by them, and purchasing CDs to participate in local experiences, encounters, and events. Furthermore, Akimoto Yasushi's vision for a network of regional idol groups was a bold attempt to reintegrate a national market that was breaking apart. As audiences were becoming more migratory and fickle in the emerging digital economy, Akimoto offered to the music and television industries a means to reconstitute the national audience through a return to the local, embodied, and affective, to interactions and relations with a particular person in a particular time and place. As we have argued elsewhere, the mass deployment and dependency on idols in Japan today suggests industries struggling to attract and hold attention in the face of challenges posed by media convergence (Galbraith and Karlin 2016: 6–7).[1]

On the other hand, in addition to overseas events, expansion beyond Japan to include sister groups in several neighboring countries has, Tim Craig argues, "challenged the assumption . . . that AKB48's appeal and business model were Japan-specific"

(Craig and Zhang 2017: 81).[2] This rings true, but AKB48's appeal and business model are not necessarily the same thing. What is spreading is more a business or franchise model than a particular idol group. Local theaters with local idols appeal to local fans to buy material products that give them privileged physical access. Furthermore, while the suggestion that AKB48 has growing international appeal seems right, this is not without friction. When Akimoto proposes that some responses to AKB48 are akin to saying "Elvis Presley shaking his hips was bad" (quoted in Craig and Zhang 2017: 83), he raises the specter of sexuality, specifically "bad sex." The inversion is striking: not the American Elvis driving women wild, but the Japanese AKB48 driving men wild by shaking their hips. Just as powerfully as they attract, so too can they repulse, or galvanize affective alliances against idols rather than with them, which points us toward the political dimensions of global circulation.

Just as fan communities and media corporations are not always or necessarily national in character, so too are affective alliances not always or necessarily contained within the borders of the nation. In the 1990s, J-pop and trendy dramas flowed from Japan to East and Southeast Asia, which contributed to the emergence of "affective media geographies" (Lamarre 2015). Idols played a significant role in this phenomenon. Looking back on the growing popularity of Japanese media in East and Southeast Asia in the 1990s, Aoyagi Hiroshi argues that idol music and television are carriers of information about "a modern, urban lifestyle that students and young working people in Asia's upward-moving economies find attractive and relevant to their own changing lives" (Aoyagi 2000: 310). From his interviews, Aoyagi draws the conclusion that idols are a "brand" that speaks to "a lifestyle of urban affluence"

(Aoyagi 2000: 323). Not only were Japanese idols becoming popular in the 1990s, but collaborations among producers and promoters also led to Asian idols being formulated on the model of Japanese idols (Aoyagi 2000: 318–21). Content was made and remade around the region, too. In a famous example, *Boys Over Flowers* (Hana yori dango, 2005) not only became a trendy drama and idol vehicle in Japan, but also was remade in Taiwan, South Korea, China, and the Philippines, with this content circulating around East and Southeast Asia and flowing back into Japan to inspire more idol content (Lamarre 2015: 95–96; also Otmazgin 2016).

While Aoyagi sees "Japan's deepening engagement with the rest of Asia," "cross-cultural affinity and influence in Asia," and "pan-Asian identity" (Aoyagi 2000: 309–10), Koichi Iwabuchi is more skeptical. In *Recentering Globalization*, Iwabuchi points out that satellite broadcasters such as Star TV were broadcasting Japanese television in Taiwan from the early 1990s, exports of Japanese television went up from 2,200 hours in 1971 ("the first year of the idol era") to 19,546 hours in 1992, and the East and Southeast Asian market received almost half of the total number of Japanese television exports by 1995 (Iwabuchi 2002: 4–5, 47).[3] The passionate consumption of idols in many parts of East and Southeast Asia led to the establishment of a government committee in Japan in 1997 (Iwabuchi 2002: 5). All of this might seem to reinforce Aoyagi's position, but Iwabuchi raises questions about Japan's so-called return to Asia, especially uneven relations and asymmetrical flows that are familiar from the days of Japanese empire (Iwabuchi 2002: 52–53, 73, 201). Indeed, much of the discourse about affective alliances in East and Southeast Asia imagines Japan displacing the United States as a new cultural center.[4] Furthermore, fans of Japanese idols in Taiwan and South Korea, former Japanese colonies, suggest the tantalizing possibility of overcoming history (Iwabuchi 2002: 53, 201). In sum, Iwabuchi shines a light on the politics behind the celebration of the powerful attraction and affect of Japanese idols in Asia in the 1990s. The celebration brought together producers, promoters, and politicians, who all had a vested interest in the success of Japanese idols. Iwabuchi highlights here a "strong nationalist impulse," which he refers to as "trans/nationalism" (Iwabuchi 2002: 52). This impulse has only become stronger since.

Writing in 2002, Iwabuchi presciently notes the rise of South Korean idol music and dramas (Iwabuchi 2002: 210), which would lead to increased nationalistic competition between Japan and its neighbor (and former colony). The very same year that Iwabuchi published *Recentering Globalization*, the South Korean idol drama *Winter Sonata* (Gyeoul yeonga) aired in its country of origin; when broadcast in Japan the following year, it generated a base of dedicated fans and became a surprise hit. The "Korean wave," which had been sweeping East and Southeast Asia, finally made its way to Japan's shores. The first wave of dramas was followed by a second wave of K-pop, which saw idols such as Girls' Generation and Kara break into the mainstream Japanese market. For some, particularly reactionaries on the right, this reverse flow of idol media from Asia to Japan in the 2000s was less comfortable than Japan's "return to Asia" in the 1990s, which came with a privileged sense of being the center, above and ahead of neighbors (Jung 2017: 184, 187, 189). While some argue that the South Korean government's decision to officially invest in national media industries in the late 1990s inspired a more proactive policy agenda in Japan (Choo 2011: 101), increased competition from South Korea in the early 2000s certainly accelerated the process.

As if to inaugurate this new era of cultural politics, in 2002, American journalist Douglas McGray published his influential article on "Japan's gross national cool," which advanced that Japan had become "a cultural superpower" and encouraged the Japanese government to harness its influence overseas (McGray 2002: 52–54). Such ideas found a receptive audience among Japanese politicians such as Kondō Sei'ichi and Asō Tarō, who became more vocal about "soft power" (Leheny 2006b: 220–29). As the policies of promoting media and popular culture as part of public diplomacy have increased in intensity, the rivalry between Japan and South Korea has become more marked. Revisiting his earlier thoughts on trans/nationalism, Iwabuchi has more recently referred to the situation in East Asia as one of "inter-nationalism," or the "reworking and strengthening of the national in tandem with the intensification of cross-border media flows" (Iwabuchi 2010: 89). In other words, Japan and South Korea, among other nations in the region, are increasingly branding themselves in terms of media and popular culture (Iwabuchi 2010: 90).

Here again we find idols. If Japan has for many been the home of idols, or "Idol Japan" (Nakamori 2007), a nation with a surplus of "idol national wealth" (Sakai 2014), then it is being challenged by the rise of South Korea as the "Idol Republic" (Kim 2011). What's more, K-pop seems to be outperforming J-pop as the new hot thing in many parts of the world. And while South Korean idols are to some extent produced to approach the North American standard of style and sound (Lie 2015: 100–09), which aids in their smooth circulation, Japanese idols are persistently understood to be somehow "different." This difference, real or imagined, has become an issue of concern in "inter-national" (in Iwabuchi's sense) circulation.

In *Recentering Globalization*, Iwabuchi argues that much of what travels from Japan to the world is "culturally odorless" (Iwabuchi 2002: 27). The provocative turn of phrase draws attention to the body, as Iwabuchi explains: "The cultural odor of a product is . . . closely associated with racial and bodily images of a country of origin" (Iwabuchi 2002: 28). A culturally odorless product, then, is one in which "a country's bodily, racial, and ethnic characteristics are erased or softened" (Iwabuchi 2002: 28). For example, anime has attracted fans around the world, but often "barely feature[s] 'Japanese bodily odor'" (Iwabuchi 2002: 28). Arguably, one of the reasons why Japanese producers, promoters, and politicians were so excited about the successes of idol music and dramas in East and Southeast Asia was because Japanese bodies were present in works that were received as Japanese and attractive as such (Iwabuchi 2002: 76). In these works, one could see the tantalizing possibility that "Japanese bodily odor" had become an alluring "fragrance" (Iwabuchi 2002: 27). However, in contrast to the situation in East and Southeast Asia, Japanese idols have long had difficulty breaking into mainstream music and media markets in North America.[5] For their many critics, something about these Japanese idols just stinks.

The trouble comes from not just language barriers, but also divergent production and promotion strategies. In global circulation, without the benefit of appearing across multiple media platforms and genres of performance simultaneously, idols lack the exposure necessary for them to be engaged intertextually. Seeing an idol for the first time outside of the media-commodity system, one does not know or care about them more than any other media performer or personality; they are not engaged intimately. Instead, the idol is judged strictly as a singer or dancer—and found to be lacking in comparison to supposedly superior performers from other parts of the world. British rocker Noel Gallagher spoke for many when, in 2012, after appearing on a Japanese television show alongside members of AKB48, he suggested that they were a talentless "manufactured girl group."[6] Even if judged not on talent, but rather attractiveness and sex appeal, these idols fail. To Gallagher, they appeared to be children "between the ages of 13–15."

This comment from Gallagher underscores another issue with the reception of Japanese idols in global circulation: appearance. Although the average age of members of the AKB48 family is between seventeen and eighteen years old, and the primary and most popular performers are in their twenties, they appeared much younger to Gallagher.[7] He is not alone in this perception, which comes from the way that AKB48 is produced, presented, and promoted as young women striving to grow and establish themselves. They often appear in modified school uniforms, sing about young love and life, and foreground their immaturity and vulnerability as they start out relatively unpolished and work hard to improve as performers and personalities (recall Chapter 7). Overall, the look of AKB48, characteristic of Japanese idols, is "cute" rather than "glamorous" or "sexy." While Japanese critics praise idols for their cuteness, which makes them approachable and "adorable" (Aoyagi 2000: 312), the aesthetic puzzles many critics outside of Japan. While the slim, toned, and exposed bodies of K-pop idols resemble those of pop divas in North America, the J-pop idol in her cute costumes seems somehow different, strange, and perhaps a little weird.

In line with much of the discourse about Japan as "other," the difference of Japanese idols quickly comes to be associated with sexual deviance. There is a cottage industry of writing about the imagined excesses and perversions of Japan, which often intersects with critiques of Japanese idols and affective economics involving them. For example, while idols such as AKB48 are successful at developing relationships with fans and moving them to make purchases, which is an entirely recognizable aspect of affective economics, relationships between idols and fans appear suspect to many observers of Japan.[8] These observers draw comparisons to the sex industry, whereby fans purchase not just physical access to and time with idols (e.g., buy a CD and shake their hands), but seemingly the idols themselves (i.e., their bodies). This is quite an imaginative leap, but the critique is especially common when the fan is an older man and the idol a younger woman. The response in the anglophone media to a scandal involving AKB48 member Minegishi Minami (again recall Chapter 7), for example, was not that the system is cruel, but rather that male fans are sexual deviants and female idols are sexually exploited.[9] The sexual violence of the relationship, imagined to exist just below the surface, is revealed to critics in stories about fans attacking idols when they cannot be "an idol for me alone."[10]

Things escalate quickly in this neo-orientalist discourse about "us" and "them" (Said 1978: 40) and their peculiar "enjoyment" (Žižek 1991: 165). If Japan is branded a nation of idols, then this can quickly transform into Japan being branded as a nation of normalized sexual exploitation of women. And because of the youth associated with idols,

Japan is further branded as a nation of normalized sexual exploitation of children. One sees this in a journalistic report on a "dark obsession" with idols, which begins with adult men gathered in a "dark venue in a sleazy Tokyo district" to fawn over a six-year-old girl and ends quoting activists and doctors warning of the dangers of normalizing sexualization of youth in Japan.[11] The aspirational model for that little girl on stage, and the economic model for her producers and fans, is identified by the journalist as AKB48. The critique is made even more explicit by Jake Adelstein, a journalist known for his reporting on organized crime in Japan:

> To some degree, the sexualization of young girls is mainstream in Japan. For example, Japan's most popular and mega-profitable all-female pop group AKB48 includes members as young as 13; and they've posed for ++sexy & semi-nude layouts in Japan's *Weekly Playboy* several times. . . . The AKB48 members are bound by their contracts to remain celibate while working for the parent company that manages the group, but they often appear in lurid commercials and videos depicting the band members exchanging kisses and singing sexually suggestive lyrics.[12]

Adelstein goes on to assert that one of the founders of AKB48 is associated with an organized crime syndicate involved in human trafficking and producing child pornography. Fact checking the often-misleading information presented does not reduce its rhetorical power or ability to incite outrage. Adelstein's description of Japan as the "Empire of Child Pornography" colors the ways that idols such as AKB48 are perceived as not an attractive aspect of Japanese media and popular culture, but rather a repulsive one.

For all of this criticism, one would think that everyone in Japan must be a fan of idols such as AKB48, but such is not the case. In his pathbreaking ethnographic fieldwork in Japan, Aoyagi reports a conversation with two female fans of idols, who imagine male fans of idols as follows: "Those people [i.e., cute-idol fans] have weird ideas about love affairs, and they are out of touch with reality. Don't you think? . . . Yeah. I think those lunatics who can be senseless enough to adore [cute-looking] idols who are much younger than they are have a serious Lolita complex. They live in their own indecent fantasies" (Aoyagi 1999: 137; bracketed qualifications in original). As much as things have changed, they have also stayed the same. Responding to the cute idols of AKB48, Matsuko Deluxe, one of the most popular media personalities in the industry today, calls these performers "shit" and their fans "disgusting male virgins."[13] When it was suggested that AKB48 might represent Japan at the opening or closing ceremonies of the Summer Olympics in Tokyo in 2020, Matsuko Deluxe retorted, "I don't care what they do, but please use somebody for the opening and closing ceremonies that wouldn't be an embarrassment."[14] Some agree that "AKB48 is the shame of Japan," while others claim that a "silent majority" opposes such idols.[15] Ultimately, for Matsuko Deluxe, AKB48 does not resonate with the "hearts of Japanese in general" or have a message that can be shared by "the people."[16] The Japanese word for "the people" (*kokumin*) is also translated as "national" when used as an adjective, as in "national idols." Matsuko Deluxe's argument, then, is that AKB48 idols are not national idols and AKB48 fans are not the people of Japan. We would do well to note the tensions of such proposed groupings, which point to contested affective alliances (fan, nation, or otherwise).

Under the banner of "Cool Japan," Japanese public diplomacy has gained much attention since the 2000s, but some wonder to whom the government is appealing. For example, AKB48 has performed at government functions with foreign dignitaries and the group's producer has had meetings with the Prime Minister of Japan, but the deployment of cute idols has raised eyebrows in North America. In a blistering critique, Laura Miller (2011) takes on Japan's "cute ambassadors" (*kawaii taishi*), or three professional performers in their twenties selected by the Ministry of Foreign Affairs to represent Japanese fashion. All are women, and one wears a schoolgirl uniform, which Miller describes as "a widely recognized object of sexual fetishization in Japan" that resonates with "global sex trafficking" (Miller 2011: 20–21). As Miller sees it, the Japanese government is a "pimp" selling the fantasy of sexually available young women, who become "fantasy-capital" for Japan in the global economy of desire (Miller 2011: 23). In a reversal of the "culturally odorless" (Iwabuchi 2002: 27–28), Japanese bodies are not erased but rather foregrounded by idols, but the production and promotion of young women as objects of desire seems problematic, as does government investment in this process. If, as Akahori Takeshi, director of the public diplomacy department at the Ministry of Foreign Affairs, suggests, "the objective is to promote an understanding of Japan, a better image, or the correct image," then the mission fails when cute idols are taken to be promoting "pedophiliac culture" (Miller 2011: 22).[17]

While raising necessary and valid issues, this focused critique of Japan perhaps obscures the dynamics of idol politics more broadly. By way of comparison, in South Korea, Yeran Kim (2011) argues that "girl industries" and "girl power" are seen as productive forces for the nation. On the one hand, "girl bodies are manufactured as cultural content and converted into economic values," and on the other hand, the "values of girl idols as cultural content are further actively promoted as national cultural resources" (Kim 2011: 335, 340). This production and promotion of young women as a national resource and content for sale on the global market might invite a critique similar to Miller's, but the South Korean government instead takes pride in the successes of K-pop idols. "In this respect," Kim explains, "girls are shifting in their social position from sexual objects of patriarchal desire into agents of patriotic nationalism, capable of bringing the nation a victory in the global cultural war" (Kim 2011: 342). Kim refers to the phenomenon of the nation celebrating girls selling on the global market as "Lolita nationalism" (Kim 2011: 342).[18]

The idea of "Lolita nationalism" no doubt raises eyebrows, but South Korean idols have escaped much of the negative criticism inspired by Japanese idols. While members of a South Korean idol group were detained entering the United States on suspicion of being "sex workers," few seem to think that South Korea, branded the "Idol Republic" (Kim 2011), has a national problem. Notably, the emphasis on age was muted in reports of the detainment.[19] This is intriguing when one considers celebration of the "Lolita" as "a sexy girl who serves the market needs of the current mediascape" (Kim 2011: 342), and that South Korean authorities have considered regulating "over-sexualized performances by teenage stars."[20] It seems that the "adult" and "mature" look of K-pop idols meets familiar expectations and hence escapes widespread criticism, which is reserved for Japan, a nation long associated in the popular imagination with sexual difference and deviance. We see here the limitations of Japanese idols in global circulation, where persistent stereotypes and expectations tend to marginalize and reject what is "other."

For his part, Iwabuchi (2002: 76) points out that "questions of what constitutes the 'real' Japan, whether it is possible to represent the 'real' faces of Japan, and in what manner such images of Japan are (in contradictory ways) consumed and received by audiences, are highly contested." This is clearly demonstrated in the fraught discussion of idols in Japan, Asia, and the world. Differences in the reception of "Japanese" idols in East and Southeast Asia and beyond, and in the 1990s and 2010s, underscore that "Japan" does not mean the same thing to all people in all places at all times. In global circulation, "Japan" can be proximate or distant, similar or different, ahead or behind the times, something to celebrate or criticize. We do not mean to resolve misunderstandings to get to the "real" Japan—which, as Iwabuchi hints at with his scare quotes, does not exist—but rather to get to the politics of imagining "Japan," as well as affective alliances with and against it. Idols open a window on to the national and "inter-national" (in Iwabuchi's sense) politics of celebrity. If, as Michael J. Wolf has suggested, "celebrity is the only currency" (Wolf 1999: 28), then we need to be sensitive to how that currency is valued in different markets. We need to take into consideration uneven relations in evaluations and asymmetrical flows. As seen in the case of AKB48 and "Japanese idols," celebrities are not created and consumed equally.

Conclusion

Toward the end of his analysis of AKB48, Sakakura Shōhei wonders if perhaps their lyrics only make sense in a particular time and place, or are "dependent on a complicated context" (Sakakura 2014: 258). In a way, the intertextuality of idols as dense carriers of meaning in a particular media-commodity system does not always translate to appreciation of their performances elsewhere (Galbraith and Karlin 2012: 12), but Sakakura seems to be suggesting something more. In the case of AKB48, perhaps their songs do not resonate with those that do not feel with the members, or move with them, in real time in Japan. Or, as Hamano Satoshi once put it to the authors, one needs to experience AKB48 live to understand. This insistence on being present, or copresence in a shared space and time, might be pointing to something that gets lost when live performances, let alone music videos, are viewed alone in front of a computer at a distance. If AKB48 teaches us anything, it is that it is precisely in a highly mediated and globalized world that one longs for the immediate and present. Fetishizes it, even. In a similar way, atomization seems to go hand in hand with desire for social interactions and relations. The story of AKB48's success speaks to the value of affective experiences at this particular conjuncture.

Over the years, many speculated that AKB48 had become a victim of its own success, or that the model of "idols that you can meet" was no longer sustainable when the now-popular group appears in the media as often if not more than it does on stage for fans. This was the standing critique in 2009, when everyone seemed sure that it was only a matter of time until AKB48 was stretched too thin, alienated fans, and subsequently imploded. At the time, people drew comparisons to Arashi and how that group of male idols was now out of reach for most fans, who were likely only to encounter their idols at crowded stadium concerts after being selected through a lottery for members of their official fan club. Ultimately, this was not the case with AKB48, because sheer numbers and the perennial replacement of idols who moved up and out of reach with fresh faces starting at the bottom and looking to build fan support meant the group continued in a relatively stable form. Members of AKB48 persisted as idols that you can meet, and as those at the top graduated, they were replaced from the existing ranks and eventually by new recruits in an endless cycle of rise and fall supported by close circles of fan patrons. It is true that few of the idols from the group's early days remained by the end of 2018, and that the most popular members do not appear on stage in Akihabara, but others do. At other stages across the country, sister groups perform. Then there are the spin-off groups and rivals, official and otherwise. In Akihabara alone, there are half a dozen stages where idol groups perform in the model of AKB48, shaking hands, selling CDs, and getting voted up and down based on fan support. More and more groups, smaller and smaller, which allow for more intimate interactions and relations. These groups are not on the same scale or as lucrative as AKB48, but they are nonetheless still part of the expanding affective economy.

Hence it is our position that AKB48 is not a victim of its own success, but rather a model that is being reproduced across Tokyo, Japan, and beyond. If there is a limit, then it is that the insistence on direct experience with another person means that the person needs to be there and not somewhere else. An image, let alone a reproduction circulating freely in the digital ether, simply will not do in this model. And so the popular members of AKB48 stand for hours at a time as hundreds, even thousands line up to see them face to face, even if only for a few seconds, look directly into their eyes, and touch them, feeling them in their presence. This means that they cannot be anywhere else, with anyone else, at that moment, which is the point really. In those moments, it is just the idol and fan, connected. A whole system exists to bring them together and capitalize on their interactions and relations, which is the story of affective economics, and it is not limited to Japan. There are other groups, other lines, but the story is much the same. If rumors are to be believed, SNH48, an idol group in Shanghai, China, that is modeled after AKB48 but broke off and became independent of Akimoto Yasushi as of 2016, is even more successful than the original.[1] In 2017, the winner of their General Election collected more votes than Sashihara Rino in Japan, and they too have an array of sister and spin-off groups. The AKB business model is spreading beyond Akimoto and Japan. There are times when it seems that everyone will be on stage, aspiring to it, or standing in the audience or in line somewhere. We will be speaking different languages, perhaps different lyrics will resonate, but the message will be the same: "I wanted to see you..."

Notes

Introduction

1 In 2017, AKB48 surpassed Hamasaki Ayumi in both single and album sales to become the most successful female artist or group and the third most successful overall, behind male artists B'z and Mr. Children.

2 Of the group's fifty-four released singles, forty-one have claimed the top spot on Oricon's singles ranking chart and thirty-six have sold over one million copies (as of November 2018).

3 As if this were not impressive enough, BTS followed it up by setting a record for most views on a video—forty-five million—in a single day with their song "Idol" on August 24, 2018. See E. Alex Jung, "BTS Speaks Out in Seoul: The K-Pop Megastars Get Candid about Representing a New Generation," *Billboard*, February 15, 2018, https://www.billboard.com/articles/news/bts/8099577/bts-interview-billboard-cover-story-2018.

4 John Lynch, "Musicians Only Got 12% of the $43 Billion the Music Industry Generated in 2017, and It Mostly Came from Touring," *Business Insider*, August 7, 2018, https://www.businessinsider.com/musicians-received-12-percent-43-billion-generated-by-music-industry-study-2018-8. See also Damon Krukowski, "How to Be a Responsible Music Fan in the Age of Streaming," *Pitchfork*, January 30, 2018, https://pitchfork.com/features/oped/how-to-be-a-responsible-music-fan-in-the-age-of-streaming/.

5 Lanier argues that like intellectuals in China during the Cultural Revolution who were sent to the countryside in order to work as farmers, musicians today are not expected to live off the labor of their creativity, but rather from revenue generated through the sale of disposable, mass-produced goods or advertising and donations.

6 International Federation of the Phonographic Industry, "Global Music Report 2018: Annual State of the Industry," April 24, 2018, https://www.ifpi.org/downloads/GMR2018.pdf.

7 Jeff Leeds, "The New Deal: Band as Brand," *The New York Times*, November 11, 2007. https://www.nytimes.com/2007/11/11/arts/music/11leed.html.

8 While early mobile downloads such as *chaku-uta full* (complete songs) promoted the consumption of singles in the 2000s, digital music sales in Japan peaked in 2009 and declined with flip phone sales, until they began to recover in the mid-2010s with the advent of streaming. See "RIAJ Yearbook 2018" and "Statistics," http://www.riaj.or.jp.

Chapter 1

1 While Steinberg is talking about anime characters, idols function in similar ways.

2 By "intertextual," we simply mean that each performance and appearance of the celebrity is read in relation to others. With idols performing and appearing across multiple genres and platforms, often simultaneously, one sees all of these performances and appearances in relation, which is to say intertextually. In this way, idols become dense carriers of information and meaning. For more, see our introduction to idols and intertextuality in Japan (Galbraith and Karlin 2012: 10–14). For a complementary discussion of celebrity, see Marshall (2002).

3 Pink Lady even released a single in the United States in 1979 that broke into Billboard's Top 40, and later went on to star in a short-lived variety show on NBC in 1980.

4 By the late 1980s, Japan had developed a heady bubble economy driven by easy money. When the Bank of Japan began to tighten liquidity, it triggered a massive decline in the stock market and crises in the banking, financial services, and real estate markets. The impact spilled over into the economy at large, leading to a reduction in full-time employment opportunities for university graduates, an eventual end to the permanent employment system, and an increase in the temporary and part-time workforce. Social problems such as "acute social withdrawal" (*hikikomori*) (Saitō 2013: 3, 83–89), increases in suicides (Leheny 2006a: 34), and decreased birth and marriage rates (Allison 2013: 33–34) characterized the trauma of the 1990s, which took on the moniker of the "lost decade."

5 Since sales of domestic music surpassed sales of foreign music in Japan in 1967 (Hosokawa 2005: 306), foreign music has been taking up a decreasing share of the market. The Recording Industry Association of Japan estimates that, on a value basis, the composition of the market for recorded music was 89 percent domestic and 11 percent international in 2016. See Recording Industry Association of Japan, "The Recording Industry in Japan: Statistics Trends," RIAJ Official Website, April 1, 2017, https://www.riaj.or.jp/f/pdf/issue/industry/RIAJ2017E.pdf.

6 This number is quite high, even for the Japanese market. In general, Japanese advertisers demand ratings of 15 to 20 percent, or about fifteen to twenty million viewers (Lukács 2010a: 40).

7   "Affective alliance" here simply means being drawn in and held close by an idol and the lifestyle or brand that they represent. For more on this concept, see the discussion of the affective economics involved in lifestyle collectivities and brand communities in Jenkins (2006: 72–79).

8   SMAP initially debuted in 1988 as a six-member group, but one of its members departed in 1996.

Chapter 2

1   For more on this dynamic, see Aoyagi (2005: 67–78).

2   "Graduation" is an affectively charged word in Japan, where it indicates institutional and life transition. The primary reference is of course school. Use of "graduation" in the idol industry makes sense, given that the youth and image of performers often overlaps with school years, but even those no longer in school can be said to graduate at a certain point in their career. In the case of idols, graduation is a euphemism for leaving a group, suspending performance activities and retiring, or transitioning into another way of life (e.g., another occupation, including homemaking). In effect, one graduates out of being an idol or part of a group.

3   The renewal of group members was not borrowed from Onyanko Club, but rather the Latin boy band Menudo (Hanayama 2014: 37).

Chapter 3

1   Quoted in Tommy Kono, "Kyary Pamyu Pamyu Shares Her Take on Minegishi Minami's Apology and Japanese Idol Culture," *AKB48 Wrap Up*, February 15, 2013, http://www.akb48wrapup.com/2013/02/kyary-pamyupamyu-shares-her-take-on-minegishi-minamis-apology-and-japanese-idol-culture-in-french-tv-show/.

2   Originally even cheaper, at the time of this writing, a ticket costs only ¥3,100 (¥2,100 for minors and women). In fact, estimated revenue does not cover the operational costs of the AKB48 Theater (Sakakura 2014: 31; also Hamano 2015). The point is not to make money on ticket sales, but to stage an encounter between idols and fans, cultivate an intimate and intense relationship between them, and then capitalize on it.

3   These impressions come from group interviews with Japanese male fans of AKB48 convened by Patrick W. Galbraith on August 14, 2010, and September 16, 2014.

4   Anna Coren, "Talk Asia: Interview with Japanese Music Producer Yasushi Akimoto," CNN, January 13, 2012, http://edition.cnn.com/TRANSCRIPTS/1201/13/ta.01.html.

5   In addition to allowing fans to choose a favorite, the large number of unique young women served as a hedge for the initial investment. Some of the young women recruited were expected to succeed, while others were not, depending on their hard work and support from fans. The passive investment strategy sought to maximize returns on investments in the long run, instead of incurring the considerable risk of committing to a single performer. At the same time, the model ensured that the group itself could go on, even if members quit (in contrast to, say, SMAP or the Beatles). Fans could shift affective alliances from one member to another, or leave along with them to be replaced by new fans of new idols.

6   This is familiar from accounts of the performance of affective alliances among fans at idols concerts, for example the practice that Aoyagi (2005: 159–64) observed of sitting down in the venue or even just leaving when one's *oshimen* is not present.

Chapter 4

1 "Net idols" are idols active primarily on the internet. As a phrase in Japanese, it refers mostly to idols with websites and blogs. It is otherwise associated with personal computers and with the late 1990s and early 2000s, before the spread of social media and micro-blogging.

2 It is not a coincidence that idols emerged in the 1970s, which is precisely when theorists observed a shift toward forms of labor dealing with the "immaterial," for example images, ideas, and information (Lazzarato 1996: 133–34). The word "immaterial," however, is something of a misnomer, because what idols such as the members of AKB48 do is material and embodied. Here, "immaterial" means images, ideas, information, feelings, experiences, and so on that cannot be reduced to the material, but are nevertheless produced by it. Idols are uniquely positioned not only as images, which nevertheless can and do affect (Hardt 1999: 96), but also as the embodied presences more often associated with affective labor.

Chapter 5

1 Anna Coren, "Talk Asia: Interview with Japanese Music Producer Yasushi Akimoto," CNN, January 13, 2012, http://edition.cnn.com/TRANSCRIPTS/1201/13/ta.01.html.

2 Akimoto likens the General Election to a kind of baseball all-star game, where the popularity of the players among fans determines participation (Akimoto and Tahara 2013: 40).

3 Much like sports teams, Akimoto conceived of each group as having a local base of fans that would fervently support their local idols (Akimoto and Tahara 2013: 19).

4   Oricon, "Nenkan CD shinguru rankingu 2010 nendo," accessed on February 25, 2019, https://www.oricon.co.jp/rank/js/y/2010/.

5   By this time, the General Election had become a media event, with results announced during a live ceremony at the Nippon Budokan stadium and streamed live to 86 theaters in Japan, as well as in Hong Kong, Taiwan, and South Korea; an estimated 150 media outlets reported on the event. See Mutsumi Morita, "No Stopping the AKB48 Juggernaut," *Daily Yomiuri Online*, June 24, 2011, http://www.yomiuri.co.jp/dy/features/arts/T11062200 2086.htm.

6   Daily Sports, "Ōshima Yūko, seken no hihan wo aete kuchi ni 'Tōhyō wa mina-san no ai'," June 9, 2011, https://web.archive.org/web/20110728095426/http://headlines.yahoo.co.jp/hl?a=20110609-00000064-dal-ent.

7   This is reinforced, and the effect amplified, by the fact that Ōshima would point to the audience from her center position on stage when performing "Heavy Rotation" live. As with "I Wanted to See You" in the AKB48 Theater before, many fans pointed back to her from their places of support in the audience.

8   Artefact, "China AKB48 Otaku Votes $150,000 for Rino Sashihara," *Sankaku Complex*, June 8, 2013, http://www.sankakucomplex.com/2013/06/08/china-akb48-otaku-votes-150000-for-rino-sashihara/.

9   Tadashi Anahori, "Strawberry Farmer Votes 4,600 for Rino Sashihara in AKB48 General Election – to No Avail!" *Tokyo Kinky*, June 10, 2014, http://www.tokyokinky.com/strawberry-farmer-votes-4600-for-rino-sashihara-in-akb48-general-election-to-no-avail/.

10 Casey Baseel, "AKB48 Fan Shows His Love the Only Way He Knows How: By Buying $300,000 Worth of CDs," *Rocket News*, May 22, 2014, http://en.rocketnews24.com/2014/05/22/akb48-fan-shows-his-love-the-only-way-he-knows-how-by-buying-300000-worth-of-cds/.

11 Rocket News, "Nai nai Okamura ga AKB48 sōsenkyō wo mondaishi 'zo tto shiteiru no boku dake?' 'osawari wa akushukai dake desho,'" June 12, 2011, http://rocketnews24.com/2011/06/12/%E3%83%8A%E3%82%A4%E3%83%8A%E3%82%A4%E5%B2%A1%E6%9D%91%E3%81%8Cakb48%E7%B7%8F%E9%81%B8%E6%8C%99%E3%82%92%E5%95%8F%E9%A1%8C%E8%A6%96%E3%80%8C%E3%82%BE%E3%83%83%E3%81%A8%E3%81%97%E3%81%A6%E3%81%84/.

Chapter 6

1 Located at the University of Birmingham, the Centre for Contemporary Cultural Studies was founded by Richard Hoggart in 1964. Among its influential researchers was Stuart Hall.

2 For the sake of clarity, this chapter will introduce only the arguments of "The Culture Industry: Enlightenment as Mass Deception." Originally published in *The Dialectic of Enlightenment* (1944), it is the core of the critique, which was later updated in solo work by Adorno (1991), who became its most noted proponent.

3 See, for example, "Four Chord Song" at: https://www.youtube.com/watch?v=5pidokakU4I.

4 Tom Barnes, "How the Music Industry Is Brainwashing You to Like Bad Pop Songs," *Mic*, August 4, 2014, https://mic.com/articles/95260/how-the-music-industry-is-brainwashing-you-to-like-bad-pop-songs#.YRXaol7Q9.

5 Along with its Sakamichi Series of "rival" sister groups—which includes Nogizaka46, Keyakizaka46, and Yoshimotozaka46—there is a grand total of 539 members (as of January 2019).

6 In view of Akimoto Yasushi's position, one cannot help but think of a statement attributed to the famously corrupt American politician Boss Tweed: "I don't care who does the electing, so long as I get to do the nominating."

7 In 2015, AKB48, sister groups SKE48 and NMB48 (from Osaka), and official "rival" Nogizaka46 (from Tokyo), took all top ten spots, except for number nine, which was a release by Arashi, the top male idol group in Japan.

8 While Jenkins notes that some fans of *American Idol* critique elections as unfair, such debates are muted in the General Election for AKB48, which is known to be dominated by those who care more and spend more money.

9 Chris Kelty gets us thinking in this direction: "If there are indeed different 'participatory cultures,' the work of explaining their differences must be done by thinking concretely about the practices, tools, ideologies, and technologies that make them up. Participation is about power, and no matter how 'open' a platform is, participation will reach a limit circumscribing power and its distribution" (quoted in Couldry and Jenkins 2014: 1108).

Chapter 7

1 Perhaps unsurprisingly, "Heavy Rotation" (2010) was at the top of Oricon's karaoke ranking for forty-eight consecutive weeks, which was a historic record (Sakakura 2014: 29).

2   Riko, "Aidoru wo 'sotsugyō' shita 43 gurūpu 364 nin no dēta kara wakatta koto wo kaku yo," Note, March 27, 2016, https://note.mu/55n0v0n/n/n2ca2e3d8caa0.

3   Furthermore, while there is a striking emphasis on amateurism in AKB48 and idols like them, it speaks to something occurring more broadly in celebrity (Dyer 1979: 42–43; Gamson 1992: 8). On the one hand, the star is an ordinary person transformed through success, but then must maintain their proximity to the audience through ritualized performances of ordinariness, for example, appearances on talk shows or posting on social media. On the other hand, stars are extraordinary in their talent, which elevates them above the ordinary, and this difference is often signified by conspicuous consumption. This difference produces stardom, but at the cost of distance from fans.

4   This might be about protecting the performers, and maintaining the fantasy of fans, but, from a structural standpoint, the policy serves to ensure that scandals involving AKB48 members do not distract from their role in advertising and promoting products and services. The production companies managing idols "face major repercussions when their stars get in trouble for personal scandal—first and foremost because companies have invested in using their 'clean' image to promote their products" (Marx 2012: 51).

5   Originally a way for companies to showcase products, the "image video" was quickly picked up by the idol industry to showcase young women (and notably retains this gender bias). Image videos are for the most part a genre of non-nude erotica, where the idol adopts various positions and poses, and, if not already in a swimsuit or underwear, strips

down to them. This is done extremely slowly, with the idol
making sure that there is ample time to see each pose from
multiple angles. Movement of the camera is interspersed
with repetitious close-ups of isolated body parts—eyes, lips,
hands, legs, buttocks, breasts.

6   Horkheimer and Adorno explain: "The culture industry
endlessly cheats its consumers out of what it endlessly
promises. The promissory note of pleasure issued by plot
and packaging is indefinitely prolonged: the promise,
which actually comprises the entire show, disdainfully
intimates that there is nothing more to come, that the diner
must be satisfied with reading the menu. . . . By constantly
exhibiting the object of desire, the breasts beneath the
sweater, the naked torso of the sporting hero, it merely
goads the unsublimated anticipation of pleasure, which
through the habit of denial has long since been mutilated
as masochism. There is no erotic situation in which
innuendo and incitement are not accompanied by the
clear notification that things will never go so far. . . . To offer
them something and to withhold it is one and the same.
That is what the erotic commotion achieves. Just because
it can never take place, everything revolves around coitus"
(Horkheimer and Adorno 2002: 111, 113).

7   From ranking number fourteen, Minegishi dropped to
eighteen. This drop was significant because it meant that
she was no longer a select member, but she still received
38,985 votes.

Chapter 8

1   Arguably, the adoption of the performative strategy
of cuteness helps to sustain and deepen the intimate

relationship between idol and fan. We are thinking here of Konrad Lorenz and his description of caregiving behavior induced in adults through the cuteness of infantile characteristics and features (Glocker et al. 2009).

2 So there is internal tension: "The housewife's description of the recipe for drama as 'getting into trouble and out again' encompasses the whole of mass culture from the weak-minded women's serial to its highest productions"; but, "For the housewife, despite the films which are supposed to integrate her further still, the dark of the cinema grants a refuge in which she can spend a few unsupervised hours, just as once, when there were still dwellings and evening repose, she could sit gazing out of the window" (Horkheimer and Adorno 2002: 111, 123).

Chapter 9

1 For her part, Lukács is aware that "the binary of empowerment and disempowerment has lost analytical force in a context in which subjectivity is the main source of valuation," or, simply, that the "conditions of exploitation [have] become more intricate" (Lukács 2013: 60). Similarly, in the case of aspiring idols and their families in South Korea, Ho Swee Lin argues that "while these dreams ultimately serve the interests of music companies who are becoming South Korea's new *chaebols* (conglomerates) and those of policymakers and bureaucrats more than those of parents, many [idols and] parents are also active agents who willingly participate in the process in the hope of gaining greater social recognition and a stronger sense of self-worth in contemporary Korean society, and not passive victims of commercial and ideological manipulations" (Ho 2012b: 499–500).

2   It should also come as very little surprise that, according to a former member of AKB48, many idols in the group struggle with mental health issues connected to being overworked and uncertain about their self-worth. See Casey Baseel, "'There Are Many Mentally Unwell Girls in AKB48' Claims Ex-Member of Japan's Top Idol Singer Group," *Sora News 24*, January 16, 2019, https://soranews24.com/2019/01/16/there-are-many-mentally-unwell-girls-in-akb48-claims-ex-member-of-japans-top-idol-singer-group/.

3   We probably should not be too shocked by this, given that Shinoda Mariko, one of the earliest members of AKB48, once tweeted that "I usually get two hours of sleep."

4   Documentary of AKB48, "Amamiya Karin-san (sakka), Takemoto Novala-san (sakka) ni komento wo itadakimashita," January 18, 2011, http://www.2010-akb48.jp/info.html.

5   Conducted in 2008, the survey asked young women between the ages of fifteen and twenty-two what are the "jobs you want to do, wanted to do, or would like to try" and found that the top three choices were actress or model; singer or musician; and entertainer, talent, or comedian. The survey was conducted by cell phone and received 1,154 responses. Respondents could choose as many occupations as they wanted, and these were the top three with 43.9 percent, 40.6 percent, and 38.1 percent, respectively.

6   Oricon News, "'AKB48 sōsenkyo' meishiin rankingu, Maeda Atsuko no rekishi-teki meigen ga ichii ni," June 5, 2015, https://www.oricon.co.jp/news/2053837/full/.

Chapter 10

1 The spectacle included, for example, creating a virtual member of AKB48 and promoting her as a dark horse contender who might just unseat Maeda and Ōshima. For more on this publicity stunt, see Amy Lee, "Aimi Eguchi, of Japan's AKB48 Pop Idols, Has a Secret: She's Not Human," *Huffington Post*, June 23, 2011, https://www.huffingtonpost.com/2011/06/23/akb48-aimi-eguchi_n_882820.html.

2 "AKB48, *anan* de hatsu no joseishi hyōshi Ōshima ga renai-kan gekihaku," eltha, August 17, 2010, https://beauty.oricon.co.jp/news/79110/full/.

3 Karube Rihito, "Watashi-tachi ga josei aidori ni hamaru riyū: Kyūzō suru 'onna-ota'-tachi," *Withnews*, August 27, 2016, https://withnews.jp/article/f0160827002qq000000000000000W02t10501qq000013900.

4 Junichi Bekku, "In the Quest for Fame, Underground Idol Groups Slog It Out with Just a Few Fans," *Asahi Shimbun*, March 31, 2015, https://ajw.asahi.com/article/cool_japan/style/AJ201503310011.

5 See the official website at: http://UNIDOL.jp/.

6 For more on UNIDOL and the spread of idol culture to Japanese universities, see Galbraith 2016. In particular, note the journey of SPH48, a cover idol group inspired by AKB48, and its struggles to perform cuteness for a critical audience.

7 Quoted in Ōnishi Motohiro, "Joshi daisei, aidoru ni naritai: Nihon ichi kettei sen ni 40 daigaku," *Asahi Shimbun*, March 16, 2015, http://www.asahi.com/articles/ASH3B5F22H3BUCVL01R.html. The connection to cover bands is suggestive. Mōri Yoshitaka points out that the band boom occurred in the 1990s, a time when Japan was undergoing an economic crisis and individuality and creativity came to be valued as part of a post-Fordist regime of flexible accumulation (Mōri 2009: 479–81).

8 "About UNIDOL," UNIDOL Official Website, accessed on February 25, 2019, http://unidol.jp/about.

9 "UNIDOL," Wikipedia, accessed February 25, 2019, https:// ja.wikipedia.org/wiki/UNIDOL.

10 Tada Copy, "UNIDOL Summer 2014," July 25, 2014, http:// www.tadacopy.com/download/2014unidol.pdf.

11 Morii Ryūjirō, "Arayuru aidoru gurūpu kyoku no dansu wo, minna de kopii shimakuru 'aikopi' ga kamii!" *Business Journal*, May 10, 2018, https://biz-journal.jp/2018/05/post_23279.html.

12 This is of course not unique to the Japanese case. Indeed, John Lie implies something similar in his discussion of South Korea's "large reserve army of potential K-pop stars" (Lie 2015: 130). In a provocative explanation of the phenomenon, Lie argues that K-pop is designed to be memorable, inspire mimicry, and spread like a meme (Lie 2015: 104–07, 145). Inescapable and catchy pop songs, karaoke machines, and social pressure to perform have prepared a "nation of singers," generated a "surplus," and made "K-pop star" into "the most desirable occupation for a young South Korean girl" (Lie 2015: 130–31). Hence just as UNIDOL participants cover idol dances, it is "not uncommon for young people (and even some old ones) to reproduce K-pop dance steps in public" (Lie 2015: 131). Beyond South Korea, Michelle Cho highlights global fans of K-pop performing cover dances, which they then upload to YouTube (Cho 2018). This participatory culture advertises the idols and supports their expanding success. The key point is that fans reproduce and contribute to the movement of idols in their labor of love, which drives the industry.

Chapter 11

1   For more, see Manabe (2015), Abe (2016), and Karlin (2016).

2   The album was eventually released on June 8, 2011.

3   "Dareka no tame ni purojekuto," *AKB48 Official Blog*, March 24, 2011, http://ameblo.jp/akihabara48/entry-10840070955.html.

4   Livedoor News, "'Haibun kangaenai no ga AKB' Seibu Dōmu LIVE de taoreteita no wa Maeda Atsuko dake de wa nakatta," August 22, 2011, http://news.livedoor.com/article/detail/5802049/.

5   Miracle Pine Rescue Project, post to Rikuzentakata City's Facebook page, accessed July 8, 2013, https://www.facebook.com/RikuzentakataCity/app_324905614239700.

6   The expression "*placebo Domingo in regione vivorum*" from Ps. 116:1-9 was chanted at funerals as a hymn to the deceased. Attendees that merely feigned grief were said to just sing the word "placebo," or be "placebo singers."

7   As opposed to donating directly to the Japanese Red Cross Society, the money entrusted to these corporations (*hōjin*) for the purposes of charitable donation are considered to be "gifts" (*zōyo*). According to Japanese tax law, money received as a gift is excluded from taxation only up to ¥1.1 million (about US$11,000). The rate of taxation is between 10 percent and 50 percent, depending on the size of the gift.

8   Although individual charitable contributions (*kifu*) in Japan are deductible up to 40 percent of one's annual income beyond a base of ¥2,000 (about US$20), the contributions of corporations are deductible without limitation.

9   Previous studies of celebrity involvement with charity have often observed a tension between self-promotion and a celebrity's sincere commitment to a particular cause (e.g., Samman et al. 2009).

10 Furthermore, the agenda of celebrities can limit or reorient the aims of a cause. For example, they might not want to take controversial positions and potentially alienate part of their fan base (Thrall et al. 2008).

Chapter 12

1 For comparison, consider the Japanese animation industry and "involution," whereby "the Japanese anime sector is sticking more than ever to its way of carrying out the anime business by concentrating on the Japanese domestic market" (Mihara 2018: 12; also Oguma 2017).

2 As of January 2019, overseas sister groups are based in Jakarta (JKT48), Bangkok (BNK48), Manila (MNL48), Ho Chi Minh City (SGO48), and Shanghai (AKB48 Team SH).

3 Building on Lukács and Iwabuchi, Thomas Lamarre also places emphasis on satellite broadcasters such as Star TV when he argues that the "coming in common" of television in East Asia was made possible by "the production of distribution" (Lamarre 2015: 117–18, 120). The expansion of communication channels outpaced the production of content, which created the conditions for rebroadcasting and remaking existing content. Japanese television, which was not thought to have much export value because of its focus of the here and now of consumer culture in Japan, provided a cheap alternative to domestic production.

4 For example, Ishihara Shintarō, a conservative and populist politician, writes glowingly of Japanese popular songs being sung in East and Southeast Asia, just as American songs were sung during and after the Occupation of Japan (Iwabuchi 2002: 66).

5   Pink Lady, Matsuda Seiko, and Utada Hikaru, some of the bestselling and most beloved idols of their respective decades, all made failed attempts at mainstream music and media debuts in North America. However, as in the case of East and Southeast Asia, there are undoubtedly fans contributing to "rogue flows" (Iwabuchi 2002: 137–40; Lamarre 2015: 114–16).

6   Arama, "Noel Gallagher Comments About AKB48," May 27, 2012, http://aramatheydidnt.livejournal.com/3845806.html.

7   AKB Fan, "AKB48 gurūpu zen membā nenrei betsu risuto (sōsenkyo bunseki raitā)," August 15, 2013, http://blog.goo. ne.jp/tedpapa/e/6f0c11b95d187c20fb836772512b8a97.

8   We should note here that just as this is not limited to Japan, it is not only male fans interacting with female idols this way. There are underground/indies male idol groups that, in exchange for purchasing CDs and other commodities, will talk with fans, hug them, and even mock kiss with only a finger separating lips (Excite News, "Menzu chika aidoru no kageki sābisu no jittai! 1 fun 1000 en de 'hagu & yubi chū' no koibito kibun," May 8, 2018, https://www.excite.co.jp/ News/entertainment_g/20180508/Messy_64357.html). This of course brings to mind hosts (Takeyama 2010).

9   See, for example, Ian Martin, "AKB48 Member's 'Penance' Shows Flaws in Idol Culture," *Japan Times*, February 1, 2013, http://www.japantimes.co.jp/culture/2013/02/01/music/ akb48-members-penance-shows-flaws-in-idol-culture/.

10   Kyodo, "Stabbed Idol in Critical Condition; Fan Faces Charge of Attempted Murder," *Japan Times*, May 22, 2016, http:// www.japantimes.co.jp/news/2016/05/22/national/crime- legal/female-idol-stabbed-multiple-times-by-purported- fan-at-event-in-western-tokyo-police/#.V0qHrWZvw7A.

11 Harumi Ozawa, "Japanese Adults Vent Dark Obsession with Young Girls at 'Little Idols' Concerts," *Japan Times*, January 30, 2018, https://www.japantimes.co.jp/news/2018/01/30/national/social-issues/japanese-adults-vent-dark-obsession-young-girls-little-idols-concerts/#.W20qtX59jfa.

12 Jake Adelstein and Angela Erika Kubo, "Japan's Kiddie Porn Empire: Bye-Bye?" *Daily Beast*, June 3, 2014, http://www.thedailybeast.com/articles/2014/06/03/japan-s-kiddie-porn-empire-bye-bye.html.

13 Crazy for Five O'clock, "Naka Riisa 'AKB renai kinshi rūru' wo hihan," February 4, 2013, https://www.youtube.com/watch?v=sDcjv8BDFZw. Livedoor, "AKB no rakkyoku wa 'ippan no Nihonjin no kokoro niwa todoite konai:' Matsuko Derakkusu ga kataru 'Mo musu' to 'AKB' no ōki na chigai towa," April 15, 2015, http://news.livedoor.com/article/detail/10008268/.

14 Rocket News, "Cross-Dressing Talent Matsuko Deluxe: AKB Opening the Tokyo Olympics 'Would Embarrass Japan,'" January 29, 2015, http://en.rocketnews24.com/2015/01/29/cross-dressing-talent-matsuko-deluxe-akb-opening-the-tokyo-olympics-would-embarrass-japan/.

15 Gee Kawai, "No to Yasushi Akimoto: Akimoto Yasushi 'gorin soshiki iinkai riji' no kiyō wo chūshi shite kudasai," Change.org, January 27, 2014, https://www.change.org/p/no-to-yasushi-akimoto.

16 Livedoor, "AKB no rakkyoku wa 'ippan no Nihonjin no kokoro niwa todoite konai:' Matsuko Derakkusu ga kataru 'Mo musu' to 'AKB' no ōki na chigai towa," April 15, 2015, http://news.livedoor.com/article/detail/10008268/.

17 Akahori is quoted in Mark Ellwood, "Japan's Ambassadors of Cute," *Financial Times*, March 27, 2010, http://www.ft.com/cms/s/2/06978f58-384d-11df-8420-00144feabdc0.html.

18 Indeed, Ho Swee Lin underscores that, in the late 2000s, "major entertainment agencies began mobilizing the local media's support and invoking nationalistic sentiment in their expansion strategies. This soon led to a 'bureaucratic turf war' in 2011, when various government agencies rushed into promoting K-pop globally, and gave the K-pop industry the official endorsement it needed to gain the recognition and respectability it has in South Korea today" (Ho 2012b: 474). For specifics on government actions, see Ho (2012b: 483–84).

19 Although nowhere near as pointed as much of the popular writing on Japanese idols, this incident was an opportunity for the journalist to critique "South Korea's K-pop scene, which has been exported with enormous success across Asia and beyond, [but] is dominated by young girl and boy bands whose members are sometimes as young as 13 or 14 years old." The story is tellingly tagged as one about "music" and "sexual offences." See ABC, "Oh My Girl: K-Pop Band Detained at Los Angeles Airport on Suspicion of Being Sex Workers, Agency Says," December 11, 2015, http://www.abc.net.au/news/2015-12-11/k-pop-band-detained-at-la-airport-as-suspected-sex-workers/7022820.

20 Global Times, "South Korea to Crack Down on Sexy Shows by Teenage Stars," October 17, 2012, http://www.globaltimes.cn/content/738997.shtml.

Conclusion

1   This speaks to the phenomenon of "China's fan economy," which is beginning to impact the charts in North America. See Adam Minter, "How to Top the Charts in China: Foreign Brands and Celebrities Need to Figure Out the Country's Unique, and Insanely Obsessive, Fan Culture," Bloomberg, November 14, 2018, https://www.bloomberg.com/opinion/articles/2018-11-14/kris-wu-beat-ariana-grande-with-help-from-china-s-fan-economy.

Bibliography

Abe, Marié. 2016. "Sounding Against Nuclear Power in Post-3.11 Japan: Resonances of Silence and Chindon-Ya," *Ethnomusicology* 60, no. 2: 233–62.

Adorno, Theodor. 1991. *The Culture Industry: Selected Essays on Mass Culture*, edited by J. M. Bernstein. London: Routledge.

Akimoto, Yasushi. 2012. "Akimoto Yasushi-shi intabyū: Naze AKB48 wa kigyō ni kiyō saretsuzukeru no ka," *Hansoku kaigi* 174: 28–31.

Akimoto, Yasushi, and Tahara Sōichirō. 2013. *AKB48 no senryaku! Akimoto Yasushi no shigoto-jutsu*. Tokyo: Asukomu.

Allison, Anne. 2009. "The Cool Brand, Affective Activism and Japanese Youth," *Theory, Culture and Society* 26, no. 2–3: 89–111.

Allison, Anne. 2013. *Precarious Japan*. Durham, NC: Duke University Press.

Ang, Ien. 1990. "Melodramatic Identifications: Television Fiction and Women's Fantasy." In *Television and Women's Culture: The Politics of the Popular*, edited by Mary Ellen Brown, 75–88. London: Sage.

Aoyagi, Hiroshi. 1999. "Islands of Eight Million Smiles: Pop-Idol Performances and the Field of Symbolic Production." PhD diss., University of British Columbia.

Aoyagi, Hiroshi. 2000. "Pop Idols and the Asian Identity." In *Japan Pop! Inside the World of Japanese Popular Culture*, edited by Timothy J. Craig, 309–26. New York: M.E. Sharpe.

Aoyagi, Hiroshi. 2005. *Islands of Eight Million Smiles: Idol Performance and Symbolic Production in Contemporary Japan*. Cambridge, MA: Harvard University Asia Center.

Attwood, Feona. 2007. "No Money Shot? Commerce, Pornography and New Sex Taste Cultures," *Sexualities* 10, no. 4 (October 1): 441–56.

Bekker, Marrie H. J., and Ad J. J. M. Vingerhoets. 2001. "Male and Female Tears: Swallowing Versus Shedding? The Relationship Between Crying, Biological Sex and Gender." In *Adult Crying: A Biopsychosocial Approach*, edited by Ad J. J. M. Vingerhoets and Randolph R. Cornelius, 91–113. London: Routledge.

Berlant, Lauren. 2011. *Cruel Optimism*. Durham, NC: Duke University Press.

Blumenthal, Dannielle. 1997. *Women and Soap Opera: A Cultural Feminist Perspective*. New York: Praeger.

Boorstin, Daniel J. 2012. *The Image: A Guide to Pseudo-Events in America*. New York: Vintage.

Brockington, Dan, and Spensor Henson. 2015. "Signifying the Public: Celebrity Advocacy and Post-Democratic Politics," *International Journal of Cultural Studies* 18, no. 4: 431–48.

Burwell, Catherine, and Megan Boler. 2008. "Calling on the Colbert Nation: Fandom, Politics and Parody in an Age of Media Convergence," *The Electronic Journal of Communication* 18, no. 2. http://www.cios.org/www/ejc/EJCPUBLIC/018/2/01845.html.

Cho, Michelle. 2018. "3 Ways that BTS and Its Fans Are Redefining Liveness," *Flow Journal*, May 29, 2018. https://www.flowjournal.org/2018/05/bts-and-its-fans/.

Choo, Kukhee. 2011. "Nationalizing 'Cool:' Japan's Global Promotion of the Content Industry." In *Popular Culture and the State in East and Southeast Asia*, edited by Nissim Otmazgin and Eyal Ben-Ari, 85–105. London: Routledge.

Chouliaraki, Lilie. 2012. "The Theatricality of Humanitarianism: A Critique of Celebrity Advocacy," *Communication and Critical/Cultural Studies* 9, no. 1: 1–21.

Condry, Ian. 2013. *The Soul of Anime: Collaborative Creativity and Japan's Media Success Story*. Durham, NC: Duke University Press.

Couldry, Nick, and Henry Jenkins. 2014. "Participations: Dialogues on the Participatory Promise of Contemporary Culture and Politics," *International Journal of Communication* 8: 1107–112.

Craig, Tim. 2017. "Japanese Pop Music and Idols." In *Cool Japan: Case Studies from Japan's Cultural and Creative Industries*, edited by Tim Craig, 25–46. Ashiya, Japan: BlueSky Publishing.

Craig, Tim, and Lauren Jubelt. 2017. "Johnny & Associates: Japanese Pop Idol Producer Faces a Changing World." In *Cool Japan: Case Studies from Japan's Cultural and Creative Industries*, edited by Tim Craig, 47–62. Ashiya, Japan: BlueSky Publishing.

Craig, Tim, and Songyu Zhang. 2017. "AKB48: The Making of a Pop Idol Juggernaut." In *Cool Japan: Case Studies from Japan's Cultural and Creative Industries*, edited by Tim Craig, 63–91. Ashiya, Japan: BlueSky Publishing.

Cretser, Gary A., William K. Lombardo, Barbara Lombardo, and Sharon Mathis. 1982. "Reactions to Men and Women Who Cry: A Study of Sex Differences in Perceived Societal Attitudes Versus Personal Attitudes," *Perceptual and Motor Skills* 55, no. 2: 479–86.

Darling-Wolf, Fabienne. 2004. "SMAP, Sex, and Masculinity: Constructing the Perfect Female Fantasy in Japanese Popular Music," *Popular Music and Society* 27, no. 3: 357–70.

De Launey, Guy. 1995. "Not-so-Big in Japan: Western Pop Music in the Japanese Market," *Popular Music* 14, no. 2: 203–25.

Dyer, Richard. 1979. *Stars*. London: British Film Institute.

Ekman, Paul, and Wallace V. Friesen. 2003. *Unmasking the Face: A Guide to Recognizing Emotions from Facial Clues*. Los Altos, CA: ISHK.

Fantone, Laura. 2005. "Precarious Changes: Gender and Generational Politics in Contemporary Italy," *Feminist Review* 87: 5–20.

Fiske, John. 1992. "The Cultural Economy of Fandom." In *The Adoring Audience: Fan Culture and Popular Media*, edited by Lisa A. Lewis, 30–49. London: Routledge.

Fiske, John. 1994. "Television Pleasure." In *Media Texts: Authors and Readers*, edited by David Graddol and Oliver Boyd-Barrett, 239–55. Philadelphia, PA: Open University Press.

Frey, William H. 1985. *Crying: The Mystery of Tears*. Minneapolis, MN: Winston Press.

Frijda, Nico H. 1986. *The Emotions*. Cambridge, United Kingdom: Cambridge University Press.

Frith, Hannah. 2015. "Visualising the 'Real' and the 'Fake': Emotion Work and the Representation of Orgasm in Pornography and Everyday Sexual Interactions," *Journal of Gender Studies* 24, no. 4: 386–98.

Fuchs, Christian. 2012. "Dallas Smythe Today: The Audience Commodity, the Digital Labour Debate, Marxist Political Economy and Critical Theory; Prolegomena to a Digital Labour Theory of Value," *Triple* 10, no. 2. http://www.triple-c.at/index.php/tripleC/article/view/443.

Furuhashi, Kenji. 1989. "C-kyū aidoru ni jinsei wo ageta seishokusha! Aidoru ga hito kara mono ni natta toki, mania ga umareta!" In *Bessatsu takarajima 104 gō: Otaku no hon*, edited by Ishii Shinji, 24–39. Tokyo: JICC shuppankyoku.

Galbraith, Patrick W., and Jason G. Karlin. 2016. "Introduction: At the Crossroads of Media Convergence in Japan." In *Media Convergence in Japan*, edited by Patrick W. Galbraith and Jason G. Karlin, 1–28. Ann Arbor, MI: Kinema Club.

Galbraith, Patrick W., and Jason G. Karlin. 2012. "Introduction: The Mirror of Idols and Celebrity." In *Idols and Celebrity in Japanese Media Culture*, edited by Patrick W. Galbraith and Jason G. Karlin, 1–32. New York: Palgrave.

Galbraith, Patrick W. 2016. "The Labor of Love: On the Convergence of Fan and Corporate Interests in Contemporary Idol Culture in Japan." In *Media Convergence in Japan*, edited by Patrick W. Galbraith and Jason G. Karlin, 232–64. Ann Arbor, MI: Kinema Club.

Gamson, Joshua. 1992. "The Assembly Line of Greatness: Celebrity in Twentieth-Century America," *Critical Studies in Mass Communication* 9: 1–24.

Gendron, Bernard. 1986. "Theodor Adorno Meets the Cadillacs." In *Studies in Entertainment: Critical Approaches to Mass Culture*, edited by Tania Modleski, 18–38. Bloomington, IN: Indiana University Press.

Glasspool, Lucy. 2012. "From Boys Next Door to Boys' Love: Gender Performance in Japanese Male Idol Media." In *Idols and Celebrity in Japanese Media Culture*, edited by Patrick W. Galbraith and Jason G. Karlin, 113–30. New York: Palgrave.

Glocker, Melanie L., Daniel D. Langleben, Kosha Ruparel, James W. Loughead, Ruben C. Gur, and Norbert Sachser. 2009. "Baby Schema in Infant Faces Induces Cuteness Perception and Motivation for Caretaking in Adults," *Ethology: Formerly Zeitschrift Fur Tierpsychologie* 115, no. 3: 257–63.

Graeber, David. 2004. *Fragments of an Anarchist Anthropology*. Chicago, IL: Prickly Paradigm Press.

Grossberg, Lawrence. 1992. "Is There a Fan in the House? The Affective Sensibility of Fandom." In *The Adoring Audience: Fan Culture and Popular Media*, edited by Lisa A. Lewis, 50–65. London: Routledge.

Hamano, Satoshi. 2012. *Maeda Atsuko wa Kirisuto wo koeta: Shūkyō toshite no AKB48*. Tokyo: Chikuma shinsho.

Hamano, Satoshi. 2015. "Shūkyō toshite no AKB48." Lecture for the Kadokawa Summer Program Research Group, the University of Tokyo, January 23.

Hanayama, Toya. 2014. *Yomu Mō-musume*. Tokyo: Koa magajin.

Hardt, Michael. 1999. "Affective Labor." *Boundary 2*, no. 26: 89–100.

Hardt, Michael, and Antonio Negri. 2004. *Multitude: War and Democracy in the Age of Empire*. New York: Penguin Press.

Hatfield, Elaine, and John T. Cacioppo. 1994. *Emotional Contagion*. Cambridge, United Kingdom: Cambridge University Press.

Hills, Matt. 2002. *Fan Cultures*. London: Routledge.

Ho, Swee Lin. 2012a. "Emotions, Desires, and Fantasies: What Idolizing Means for Yon-sama Fans in Japan." In *Idols and Celebrity in Japanese Media Culture*, edited by Patrick W. Galbraith and Jason G. Karlin, 166–81. New York: Palgrave.

Ho, Swee Lin. 2012b. "Fuel for South Korea's 'Global Dreams Factory:' The Desires of Parents Whose Children Dream of Becoming K-Pop Stars," *Korea Observer* 43, no. 3: 471–502.

Horkheimer, Max, and Theodor Adorno. 2002. "The Culture Industry: Enlightenment as Mass Deception." In *Dialectic of Enlightenment: Philosophical Fragments*, edited by Gunzelin Schmid Noerr, 94–136. Stanford, CA: Stanford University Press.

Hosokawa, Shūhei. 2005. "Popular Entertainment and the Music Industry." In *A Companion to the Anthropology of Japan*, edited by Jennifer Robertson, 297–313. Oxford, United Kingdom: Blackwell Publishing.

Iwabuchi, Koichi. 2001. "Becoming 'Culturally Proximate': The A/Scent of Japanese Idol Dramas in Taiwan." In *Asian Media Productions*, edited by Brian Moeran, 54–74. London: Routledge.

Iwabuchi, Koichi. 2002. *Recentering Globalization: Popular Culture and Japanese Transnationalism*. Durham, NC: Duke University Press.

Iwabuchi, Koichi. 2010. "Undoing Inter-national Fandom in the Age of Brand Nationalism." In *Mechademia 5: Fanthropologies*, edited by Frenchy Lunning, 87–96. Minneapolis, MN: University of Minnesota Press.

Jenkins, Henry. 1992. *Textual Poachers: Television Fans and Participatory Culture*. London: Routledge.

Jenkins, Henry. 2006. *Convergence Culture: Where Old and New Media Collide*. New York: New York University Press.

Jung, Eun-Young. 2017. "Korean Pop Music in Japan: Understanding the Complex Relationship between Japan and

Korea in the Popular Culture Realm." In *Introducing Japanese Popular Culture*, edited by Alisa Freedman and Toby Slade, 180–90. London: Routledge.

Karlin, Jason G. 2012. "Through a Looking Glass Darkly: Television Advertising, Idols, and the Making of Fan Audiences." In *Idols and Celebrity in Japanese Media Culture*, edited by Patrick W. Galbraith and Jason G. Karlin, 72–93. New York: Palgrave.

Karlin, Jason G. 2016. "Precarious Consumption After 3/11: Television Advertising in Risk Society." In *Media Convergence in Japan*, edited by Patrick W. Galbraith and Jason G. Karlin, 30–59. Ann Arbor, MI: Kinema Club.

Kelly, Bill. 1998. "Japan's Empty Orchestras: Echoes of Japanese Culture in the Performance of Karaoke." In *The Worlds of Japanese Popular Culture: Gender, Shifting Boundaries and Global Cultures*, edited by Dolores Martinez, 75–87. Cambridge, United Kingdom: Cambridge University Press.

Kijima, Yoshimasa. 2012. "Why Make E-*moe*-tional Attachments to Fictional Characters? The Cultural Sociology of the Post-Modern." In *Pop Culture and the Everyday in Japan: Sociological Perspectives*, edited by Katsuya Minamida and Izumi Tsuji, 149–70. Melbourne, Australia: Trans Pacific Press.

Kim, Yeran. 2011. "Idol Republic: The Global Emergence of Girl Industries and the Commercialization of Girl Bodies," *Journal of Gender Studies* 20, no. 4: 333–45.

Kimura, Tatsuya. 2007. "History of Japanese Idols: From the Silver Screen to the Internet Via the Living Room," *High Fashion: Bimonthly Magazine for Women and Men* 313: 259–60.

Kinsella, Sharon. 1995. "Cuties in Japan." In *Women, Media, and Consumption in Japan*, edited by Lise Skov and Brian Moeran, 220–54. Honolulu, HI: University of Hawai'i Press.

Kinsella, Sharon. 2014. *Schoolgirls, Money and Rebellion in Japan*. London: Routledge.

Kitagawa, Masahiro. 2013. *Yamaguchi Momoe → AKB48: A・I ・DO・RU ron*. Tokyo: Takarajimasha shinsho.

Kobayashi, Yoshinori, Nakamori Akio, Uno Tsunehiro, and Hamano Satoshi. 2012. *AKB48 hakunetsu ronsō*. Tokyo: Gentōsha.

Kon, Hiroyuki. 2012. "AKB48 kiyō no kigyō kyanpēn no uragawa: Ezaki Glico Aisu no Mi," *Hansoku kaigi* 174: 32–33.

Lamarre, Thomas. 2015. "Regional TV: Affective Media Geographies," *Asiascape: Digital Asia* 2: 93–126.

Lanier, Jaron. 2011. *You Are Not a Gadget: A Manifesto*. New York: Vintage.

Lazzarato, Maurizio. 1996. "Immaterial Labor." In *Radical Thought in Italy: A Potential Politics*, edited by Paolo Virno and Michael Hardt, 133–47. Minneapolis, MN: University of Minnesota Press.

Leheny, David. 2006a. *Think Global, Fear Local: Sex, Violence, and Anxiety in Contemporary Japan*. Ithaca, NY: Cornell University Press.

Leheny, David. 2006b. "A Narrow Place to Cross Swords: 'Soft Power' and the Politics of Japanese Popular Culture in East Asia." In *Beyond Japan: The Dynamics of East Asian Regionalism*, edited by Peter J. Katzenstein and Takashi Shiraishi, 211–37. Ithaca, NY: Cornell University Press.

Lie, John. 2015. *K-Pop: Popular Music, Cultural Amnesia, and Economic Innovation in South Korea*. Oakland, CA: University of California Press.

Lukács, Gabriella. 2010a. *Scripted Affects, Branded Selves: Television, Subjectivity and Capitalism in 1990s Japan*. Durham, NC: Duke University Press.

Lukács, Gabriella. 2010b. "Dream Labor in the Dream Factory: Japanese Commercial Television in the Era of Market Fragmentation." In *Television, Japan, and Globalization*, edited by Mitsuhiro Yoshimoto, Eva Tsai, and JungBong Choi, 173–94. Ann Arbor, MI: University of Michigan Press.

Lukács, Gabriella. 2013. "Dreamwork: Cell Phone Novelists, Labor, and Politics in Contemporary Japan," *Cultural Anthropology* 28, no. 1: 44–64.

Lukács, Gabriella. 2015. "The Labor of Cute: Net Idols, Cute Culture, and the Digital Economy in Contemporary Japan," *Positions: Asia Critique* 23, no. 3: 487–513.

Lutz, Tom. 1999. *Crying: The Natural and Cultural History of Tears*. New York: W. W. Norton & Company.

Macias, Patrick, and Tomohiro Machiyama. 2004. *Cruising the Anime City: An Otaku Guide to Neo Tokyo*. Berkeley, CA: Stone Bridge Press.

Madge, Leila. 1998. "Capitalizing on 'Cuteness:' The Aesthetics of Social Relations in a New Postwar Japanese Order," *Japanstudien* 9, no. 1: 155–74.

Manabe, Noriko. 2015. *The Revolution Will Not Be Televised: Protest Music After Fukushima*. Oxford, United Kingdom: Oxford University Press.

Marshall, P. David. 2002. "The New Intertextual Commodity." In *The New Media Handbook*, edited by Dan Harries, 69–81. London: British Film Institute.

Marx, W. David. 2012. "The *Jimusho* System: Understanding the Production Logic of the Japanese Entertainment Industry." In *Idols and Celebrity in Japanese Media Culture*, edited by Patrick W. Galbraith and Jason G. Karlin, 35–55. New York: Palgrave.

McGray, Douglas. 2002. "Japan's Gross National Cool," *Foreign Policy* 130: 44–54.

Mihara, Ryotaro. 2018. "Involution: A Perspective for Understanding Japanese Animation's Domestic Business in a Global Context," *Japan Forum*, 1–24.

Miller, Laura. 2011. "Cute Masquerade and the Pimping of Japan," *International Journal of Japanese Sociology* 20: 18–29.

Minami, Hiroshi. 1979. "Nihon no ryūkōka." In *Ryūkōka no himitsu*, edited by Katō Kōji and Tsukuda Jitsuo, 130–33. Tokyo: Bunwa shobō.

Minami, Hiroshi. 2012. "Nihon no ryūkōka." In *Bunka shakaigaku kihon bunkenshū 11: Yume to omokage*, edited by Shisō no Kagaku Kenkyūkai, 164–65. Tokyo: Chūōkōronsha.

Miura, Atsushi, and Yanauchi Tamao. 2008. *Onna wa naze kyabajō ni naritai no ka? 'Shōnin saretai jibun' no jidai*. Tokyo: Kōbunsha.

Modleski, Tania. 1986. "The Terror of Pleasure: The Contemporary Horror Film and Postmodern Theory." In *Studies in Entertainment: Critical Approaches to Mass Culture*, edited by Tania Modleski, 155–66. Bloomington, IN: Indiana University Press.

Mōri, Yoshitaka. 2009. "J-Pop: From the Ideology of Creativity to DiY Music Culture," *Inter-Asia Cultural Studies* 10, no. 4: 474–88.

Morikawa, Kaichirō. 2003. *Shuto no tanjō: Moeru toshi Akihabara*. Tokyo: Gentōsha.

Nagaike, Kazumi. 2012. "Johnny's Idols as Icons: Female Desire to Fantasize and Consume Male Images." In *Idols and Celebrity in Japanese Media Culture*, edited by Patrick W. Galbraith and Jason G. Karlin, 97–112. New York: Palgrave.

Nakamori, Akio. 2007. *Aidoru Nippon*. Tokyo: Shinchōsha.

Negri, Antonio. 1999. "Value and Affect," *Boundary 2* 26, no. 2: 77–88.

Oguma, Eiji. 2017. "An Industry Awaiting Reform: The Social Origins and Economics of Manga and Animation in Postwar Japan," *Japan Focus* 15, no. 1. https://apjjf.org/2017/09/ Oguma.html.

Okada, Toshio. 2008. *Otaku wa sude ni shinde iru*. Tokyo: Shinchōsha.

Okajima, Shinshi, and Okada Yasuhiro. 2011. *Gurūpu aidoru shinka ron: 'Aidoru sengoku jidai' ga yatte kita!* Tokyo: Mainichi komyunikēshonzu.

Okiyama, Sumihisa. 2007. "The Story of Dreams and Yearnings: The 'Promide' Picture of Marubelldo," *High Fashion: Bimonthly Magazine for Women and Men* 313: 260.

Onozawa, Shiho. 2013. "J-POP ni okeru Nihongo no kenkyū: Gendai ryūkōka no kashi ni miru tokuchō," *Kokubun* 119: 61–73.

Ōta, Shōichi. 2011. *Aidoru shinka ron: Minami Saori kara Hatsune Miku, AKB48 made*. Tokyo: Chikuma shobō.

Otmazgin, Nissim. 2016. "A New Cultural Geography of East Asia: Imagining a 'Region' through Popular Culture," *Japan Focus* 14, no. 5. http://apjjf.org/2016/07/Otmazgin.html.

Ōtsuka, Eiji. 2004. *'Otaku' no seishin shi: 1980-nendai ron*. Tokyo: Kōdansha gendai shinsho.

Paasonen, Susanna. 2010. "Labors of Love: Netporn, Web 2.0 and the Meanings of Amateurism," *New Media and Society* 12, no. 8: 1297–312.

Parc, Jimmyn, and Nobuko Kawashima. 2018. "Wrestling with or Embracing Digitization of the Music Industry: The Contrasting Business Strategies of J-Pop and K-Pop," *Kritika Kultura* 30: 28–48.

Prusa, Igor. 2012. "Megaspectacle and Celebrity Transgression in Japan: The Sakai Noriko Media Scandal." In *Idols and Celebrity in Japanese Media Culture*, edited by Patrick W. Galbraith and Jason G. Karlin, 56–71. New York: Palgrave.

Ravindran, Thara, Alton Yeow Kuan Chua, and Dion Hoe Lian Goh. 2014. "Antecedents and Effects of Social Network Fatigue," *Journal of the Association for Information Science and Technology* 65, no. 11: 2306–20.

Said, Edward. 1978. *Orientalism*. New York: Vintage Books.

Saitō, Tamaki. 2013. *Hikikomori: Adolescence Without End*, translated by Jeffrey Angles. Minneapolis, MN: University of Minnesota Press.

Sakai, Masayoshi. 2014. *Aidoru kokufu ron: Seiko, Akina no jidai kara AKB, Momokuro jidai made toku*. Tokyo: Tōyō keizai shinpōsha.

Sakakura, Shōhei. 2014. *AKB48 to burakku kigyō*. Tokyo: Iisuto puresu.

Samman, Emma, Eilish McAuliffe, and Malcolm MacLachlan. 2009. "The Role of Celebrity in Endorsing Poverty Reduction through International Aid," *International Journal of Nonprofit and Voluntary Sector Marketing* 14: 137–48.

Sayawaka. 2013. *AKB shōhō towa nani datta no ka?* Tokyo: Taiyō tosho.

Smythe, Dallas W. 1981. *Dependency Road: Communications, Capitalism, Consciousness, and Canada*. Norwood, NJ: Ablex Publishing.

Steinberg, Marc. 2012. *Anime's Media Mix: Franchising Toys and Characters in Japan*. Minneapolis, MN: University of Minnesota Press.

Tada, Michitarō. 1990. *Shigusa no Nihon bunka*. Tokyo: Kadokawa shoten.

Takahashi, Eiki (dir). 2012. *Documentary of AKB48 Show Must Go On: Shōjo-tachi wa kizutsukinagara, yume wo miru*. Tokyo: Tōhō.

Takahashi, Eiki (dir). 2013. *Documentary of AKB48 No Flower Without Rain: Shōjo-tachi wa namida no ato ni nani wo miru?* Tokyo: Tōhō.

Takahashi, Eiki (dir). 2014. *Documentary of AKB48 The Time Has Come: Shōjo-tachi wa, ima, sono senaka ni nani wo omou?* Tokyo: Tōhō.

Takeyama, Akiko. 2005. "Commodified Romance in a Tokyo Host Club." In *Genders, Transgenders and Sexualities in Japan*, edited by Mark McLelland and Romit Dasgupta, 200–15. London: Routledge.

Takeyama, Akiko. 2010. "Intimacy for Sale: Masculinity, Entrepreneurship, and Commodity Self in Japan's Neoliberal Situation," *Japanese Studies* 30, no. 2: 231–46.

Tanaka, Hidetomi. 2010. *AKB48 no keizaigaku*. Tokyo: Asahi shimbun shuppan.

Terranova, Tiziana. 2000. "Free Labor: Producing Culture for the Digital Economy," *Social Text* 18, no. 2: 33–58.

Thrall, A. Trevor, Jaime Lollio-Fakhreddine, Jon Berent, Lana Donnelly, Wes Herrin, Zachary Paquette, Rebecca Wenglinski, and Amy Wyatt. 2008. "Star Power: Celebrity Advocacy and the Evolution of the Public Sphere," *The International Journal of Press/Politics* 13, no. 4: 362–85.

Tsunku. 2000. *Rabu ron.* Tokyo: Shinchōsha.

Van Hemert, Dianne A., Fons J. R. van de Vijver, and Ad J. J. M. Vingerhoets. 2011. "Culture and Crying: Prevalences and Gender Differences," *Cross-Cultural Research* 45, no. 4: 399–431.

West, Mark D. 2006. *Secrets, Sex, and Spectacle: The Rules of Scandal in Japan and the United States.* Chicago, IL: University of Chicago Press.

Wolf, Michael J. 1999. *The Entertainment Economy: How Mega-Media Forces Are Transforming Our Lives.* New York: Three Rivers Press.

Yano, Christine. 2002. *Tears of Longing: Nostalgia and the Nation in Japanese Popular Song.* Cambridge, MA: Harvard University Asia Center.

Yano, Christine. 2004. "Letters from the Heart: Negotiating Fan-Star Relationships in Japanese Popular Music." In *Fanning the Flames: Fans and Consumer Culture in Contemporary Japan,* edited by William W. Kelly, 41–58. Albany, NY: State University of New York Press.

Žižek, Slavoj. 1991. *Looking Awry: An Introduction to Jacques Lacan through Popular Culture.* Cambridge, MA: MIT Press.

Index